Accept
the
Challenge

Accept
the
Challenge

101 STRATEGIES FOR PERSONAL SUCCESS

William P. Abram

LONGSTREET
Atlanta, Georgia

Published by
Longstreet Press
2974 Hardman Court
Atlanta, Georgia 30305

Printed in The United States of America

1st printing, 2003

Library of Congress Catalog Card Number: 2003100402

ISBN: 1-56352-721-9

This book is dedicated to my wife, Martha, whose loyalty and support are my constant source of encouragement.

THE CHALLENGE

❧ ❧

Several years ago, I hired a man to do public relations work for my company, AMC Global Communications, Inc. During his tenure, he kept urging me to get involved with broadcast radio, and we often reflected on the continuous negative babble coming from the media. My feeling was that in the midst of this steady stream of negativism, a program delivering positive reinforcement would be well received by the listening public.

As our conversations continued, a realization began to take shape: people are not only tabloid readers but also tabloid listeners. And out of these discussions came a concept called "MOTIVATIONAL MINUTES." My idea was to distill the thinking of great minds in all walks of life, past and present, into 60-second capsules that would be easy to understand.....

     .....quick and to the point.....
        .....hard hitting truth, simply stated.....
           .....Proven concepts and counsel.

These would be uplifting ideas providing positive reinforcement for people in all walks of life who are constantly exposed to the cacophony of negative babble. Most importantly, every message would be carefully crafted so as to become a powerful tactic in an individual's struggle for achievement and success.

Shortly thereafter, my PR man arranged a meeting with the station manager of WCNN in Atlanta, Georgia. He listened to my ideas and then asked whether I could write and record three "Motivational Minutes," which I did. After he listened to the tape he asked me to do three more. He then invited me to do them on a regular basis: five per week, each program to be played at different times of the day, each weekday.

Several weeks into the airing of "Motivational Minutes," I received this letter from the station manager:

RE: Motivational Minutes

Dear Bill,

I just wanted to drop you a note to let you know how pleased the staff and I are with the response to your Motivational Minutes radio program. It is one of the best-received shows of its type that I have ever been associated with in my forty or so years in radio.

It certainly seems to be something that is desperately needed as a positive alternative to the negatives that are so pervasive today.

Looking forward to a continued long association with both you and Motivational Minutes.

Very truly yours,
C.B. "Rik" Rogers

This letter together with hundreds of others and requests for copies of the messages convinced me there was a large audience who would listen to and benefit from the program.

The following pages are a collection of these broadcasts that were aired on WCNN and the Southern Radio News Network. Further, my plan has been to publish 101 of the programs under the title *101 Strategies For Personal Success*.

Finally, as a preface to these messages, the following thoughts are meant to focus on what can be the result of absorbing and then applying these powerful concepts to your personal circumstances. This should strongly encourage you to take the necessary action, for it will enormously enrich your life.

STEPS TOWARD EXCELLENCE

❧ ❧

If you are like most people, you are restlessly searching for meaning in your life. You constantly look to improve the quality of your life, to increase your personal productivity and your level of achievement. This is the challenge that every person faces. These Motivational Minutes focus on techniques and strategies to help you achieve your highest expectations and noblest dreams. They will seek to meet the challenge of providing the many insights necessary to enhance your effectiveness in every area of your life.

These messages enable you to discover (or uncover, if you will) what talents you have and how to mobilize them to unlock your ability to excel. In a keenly competitive world where competition is getting tougher, we offer you an opportunity to discover the motivation necessary to empower yourself toward greater achievement. These messages offer you specific strategies that will guarantee you greater success.

With the ability and desire to raise your level of achievement through maximizing the unused power within you will come greater recognition, better paying jobs, a heightened sense of selfworth and positions of authority in the business world. The "STRATEGIES FOR SUCCESS" learned in these Motivational Minutes will manifest themselves through increased income and broader positive opportunities in every area of your life.

Accept
the
Challenge

It is better to be
PREPARED
for an
OPPORTUNITY
and not have one,
than to have an
OPPORTUNITY
and not be
PREPARED.

—Whitney Young, Jr.

THE POWER OF THE INDIVIDUAL

❧ ❧

Highly industrialized societies like ours, with computers and robots replacing functions previously performed by people, have a definite dehumanizing effect.

Fulton Oursler wrote a book titled *What One Man Can Do*. Each chapter tells the story of an individual overcoming insuperable odds to succeed. Perhaps this is the type of thinking that gave birth to the ancient Chinese proverb: "It is better to light a candle than to curse the darkness."

Every great movement, every great idea was given birth by one individual. Do not underestimate the power that lies within you. Your abilities, your talents, your wisdom applied vigorously to any challenge will enable you to succeed.

Tom Hopkins, the great corporate trainer, suggests, do not complain about the talents that you do NOT have. Take the talents you DO have and get what you want.

...there is no

EFFORT

without error

and

SHORTCOMINGS

—THEODORE ROOSEVELT

KEYS TO SUPERIOR ACHIEVEMENT

❧ ❧

Have you ever wondered why certain people achieve so much more than others?!? Is it the superior intelligence? Or superior ability? Or superior talents?
Not at all. Here are three vital steps to superior achievement.

First, superior achievers acquire a database. They accumulate and store knowledge in their brains. They saturate themselves with information. They study constantly.

Secondly, superior achievers learn how to focus. This means they concentrate a little bit more. Focus equals concentration and intensity. Intensity involves channeling enormous amounts of energy into the task at hand (whatever that task might be).

Third, superior achievers make a commitment to excellence. They commit to being the best. Vince Lombardi said it best, "Your success in life will be in direct proportion to your commitment to excellence no matter what your chosen field."

Those of us who
REFUSE TO RISK
and grow,
GET SWALLOWED
up by life.

—Patty Hansen

THE SECRET TO SUCCESS

❧ ❧

Have you ever wondered why so few people are financially successful? Brian Tracy states that only 5 percent or less achieve financial security, needing someone to care for them at the end. The answer is: THEY HAVE NO PLAN. Failure to plan is a plan to fail! Poverty needs no plan.

In his book *The Seven Habits of Highly Effective People*, Stephen Covey says, "Begin With The End In Mind." He suggests careful planning in the form of goals for every aspect of life. No contractor begins any construction without detailed plans. Should life be any different?

Most people's lives are like rudderless ships, having no directional control! Your first step towards success is this: TAKE CHARGE OF YOUR LIFE. You do this by taking control of the information you put in your mind. Remember, "YOU BECOME WHAT YOU THINK!"

The ideas, beliefs, and plans you put in your mind will determine the degree of your success. Perhaps the New Testament said it best: "As a man thinketh in his heart, so is he."

Man must cease
ATTRIBUTING
his problems to his
ENVIRONMENT
and learn again to
EXERCISE
his free will—his
personal
RESPONSIBILITY
in the realm of faith
and morals.

—DR. ALBERT SCHWEITZER

THE FUTURE IS YOURS

Many people feel there is no future for them, the country, or even the world. The reason is

day by day...

week after week...

year after year...

people are fed this dismal concept by TV, radio and newspapers.

People forget that the media by its very nature are purveyors of negative news. In fact, the news media appear to strain to find something negative in every news story no matter how positive that story might be.

In the face of this negativism, I can guarantee you that right at this moment in your life...

in the world and....

in the country....

there are more opportunities....

more success stories...

more entrepreneurs than ever ...

before in the history of the country ... and you have been given talents, skills and abilities to take advantage of any number of opportunities that are coming your way.

Have the courage to commit yourself to a goal, any positive goal. Then take steps to achieve it. Use whatever abilities you have to reach your best potential ... your finest destiny. Your future is in your hands. It will be as good as you make it. Only remember,

Believe in yourself when no one else does.

Whatever else
HISTORY MAY
say about me when
I AM GONE,
I hope it will record
that I appealed to your
BEST HOPES,
not your worst fears;
to your
CONFIDENCE
rather than your doubts.

—FORMER PRESIDENT
RONALD REAGAN

THE IMPORTANCE OF CHANGE

❧ ❧

Have you ever noticed how people resist change?!? Most people want to maintain the status quo because it is easier and more comfortable.

Let me tell you about change.
Change frequently involves pain!!
    It involves discomfort.
        It involves stepping out into the unknown.
It may involve moving to a new part of the country,
    learning a new skill,
        developing an understanding of a new industry,
            making new friends,
                dealing in business with entirely new people.

All of this is difficult. Yet, we must remember change is the only means by which we grow as human beings.
No change means no growth...
    ...no broadening of horizons...
    ...no opening up of new vistas.
No change means settling into the same old comfortable rut because it is safe and without risk. It is painless!

My advice is: Don't resist change!

In a world that rewards change permit me to urge you to reach out for that new horizon without fear. It will transform your life into one of growth and excitement.

Society
IS ALWAYS
taken by
SURPRISE
at any new
EXAMPLE OF
common sense.

—RALPH WALDO EMERSON

ATTITUDE

❧ ❧

W. Clement Stone structured an entire company around a single concept. He called it PMA, meaning "positive mental attitude." A positive mental attitude is a pre-requisite for success.

As a matter of fact, success is a result of 85 percent attitude and 15 percent education and grade level. Of the top CEOs in the country 94 percent have developed a positive mental attitude. It is the secret to a winning way of life. Winners have an attitude of self expectancy. They expect the best! They manufacture positive results.

Where do attitudes come from? They come from expectations. If you expect to succeed more often than not, you will. If you are a salesperson you will find that people are persuaded much more by attitude than logic. Who can resist enthusiasm, excitement, optimism?

The last and most important aspect of attitude is optimism. Optimism is the belief that our own abilities are superior to the obstacles that logically should overcome us.

People are far more
PERSUADED
by the depths of
YOUR BELIEFS
and emotions than any
AMOUNT OF
logic or knowledge
you possess.

—DR. MICHAEL LeBOEUF

PEAK PERFORMERS

❧ ❧

Let me share with you some ideas from an outstanding book written by Charles Garfield entitled *Peak Performers: The New Heroes of American Business*. In his excellent study of peak performers in every walk of life Mr. Garfield discovered the following interesting characteristics:

First, he found ordinary people became peak performers when they discover something to which they can make a commitment. When they get involved in a job or a project where they feel that what they do really matters. He observed that peak performance always begins with a commitment to a mission.

Secondly, he discovered that once this ordinary person becomes a peak performer he never stops searching and learning. He becomes a student for the rest of his life. He makes a conscious decision to excel in what he is doing ... to be the best that he can be.

So, if you want to be a peak performer, a person who accomplishes great things, find that niche in life to which you can make a commitment and then become a restless searcher for knowledge and information. As a peak performer your life will become exciting and meaningful because you will move into the future constantly generating new challenges ... living with a sense that there is always more work to be done. What can be more fulfilling than this?!

Self-confidence
is the
FIRST REQUISITE
to great
UNDERTAKINGS.

—Samuel Johnson

THE WISDOM OF GOALS

❧ ❧

Maybe you have noticed how most people spend more time worrying about the future than planning for it! This pinpoints a chronic human flaw that can only be corrected by mobilizing all one's individual powers.

You see, you always have a choice. You can condemn yourself to mediocrity or you can "unlock your ability to excel." Or as Goethe put it, you can release "the genius, power and magic in ourselves."

Let me help you make your choice! It is really very simple. Tom Hopkins calls the answer "the most necessary skill of all." What is it? Goals and goal setting. Your goals are your master plan for life.

Let's talk about it. A goal is not a goal unless it is in writing. It is not a goal unless it is specific. It must be believable. Goals must encompass every area of life – career, family and spiritual well-being.

They are a lifelong commitment to growth, ever changing as we move into each new year of our lives. But most important of all, they must be vivid, exciting and challenging. Dr. Norman Vincent Peale put it this way: " If you aim at the moon, the least you can do is land among the stars."

We cannot
DEFEND FREEDOM
abroad by
DESERTING
it at home.

—Edward R. Morrow

WINNERS AND LOSERS – THE DIFFERENCE

❧ ❧

From every media source today modern man is deluged with negatives. Is it any wonder that many of us are guilty of negative thinking about our future, our opportunities and our abilities?!? Perhaps this is why many people live lives of quiet desperation. This could also be the reason why people are more inclined to say "I can't" than "I can."

Here are the risks of negative thinking. Negative thinking excuses our failures. It allows us to avoid challenges. It saps positive mental energy. It places road blocks on the road to successful careers.

If, in fact, Napoleon Hill is correct when he says "you become what your think," it is important, therefore, to say "I can" instead of "I can't" whenever you are faced with an opportunity, a challenge or a problem.

The difference between winners and losers is that winners cultivate positive thoughts, and losers cultivate negative ones.

> Losers say "I can't."
> Winners say "I can..."

...in the face of every opportunity, every problem, every challenge.

It is better
TO LIGHT
a candle than
TO CURSE
the darkness.

—ANCIENT CHINESE PROVERB

DO WHAT YOU ENJOY

❧ ❧

One of life's most difficult decisions is deciding what you want out of it. This is particularly true of career choices. Many put in their time just to receive a weekly paycheck ... trapped in jobs they dislike intensely.

The people who enjoy their jobs are living to work, not working merely to live. Seek a career you enjoy, remembering Tom Peters observation, "People rarely succeed at anything unless they enjoy it."

Only you can decide what you want. You can't delegate this decision. No one can make this decision for you. Your decision will either limit or expand your horizons.

Decisions begin with beliefs. Your beliefs become your realities ... which in turn impact on your every decision. Therefore, develop the mindset embodied in this statement "Whatever you can conceive
                and believe...
                ...you can achieve."

19

Where there is
NO VISION,
the people
PERISH.

—THE BIBLE

THE POWER OF CARING

❧ ❧

I found a very interesting concept in a book written by Zig Ziglar, the famous corporate sales trainer. He wrote, "You can get everything in life you want if you will just help enough other people get what they want."

In a world that seems motivated by greed, where most say, "Number one comes first," a corporate business trainer is offering what might be considered spiritual advice.

Another famous corporate trainer put these words in his best selling book: "I have more fun and enjoy more financial success when I stop trying to get what I want and start helping other people get what they want."

What we are talking about here is "caring." Caring is a very powerful word. People can almost always tell if you care. Maybe we are rediscovering an ancient principle which says, "Give and it shall be given unto you."

It seems the mark of success is to be a person who, in a world that is wrapped up in itself, is concerned about the welfare of other people. Another contemporary author puts it in modern perspective when he says "People do not care how much you know until they know how much you care."

Whatever you
CAN CONCEIVE
and believe, you
CAN ACHIEVE.

—Napoleon Hill

DON'T FEAR FAILURE

One of life's most important laws is:
WE CANNOT PERMIT FAILURE TO DEFEAT US.
R.H. Macy went bankrupt three times before he succeeded. Henry Ford went bankrupt in his first year in the auto business and two years later his second company failed.

Thomas Edison was asked about his thousands of failed experiments in attempting to invent the light bulb. Was he discouraged? "No," he replied, "because I have merely discovered the thousands of ways that it would not work."

Most people do not start that business they always dreamed about.

...write that book they always thought of writing...

...or put that goal on paper that has always been a vague dream, because they are afraid that they will fail.

Every accomplishment worth attempting involves the risk of failure. Many failures will precede the accomplishment of every goal.

The advice of Harvey Mackay sums it up best. "Measure success by success, not by the number of failures it takes to achieve it ... Tolerate failure. It is the price of success."

If you aim at
THE MOON,
the least you
CAN DO IS
land among
THE STARS.

—DR. NORMAN VINCENT PEALE

DISCIPLINE DETERMINATION
AND DETAIL

❧ ❧

Possibly you have noticed in your travels how some people seem destined to succeed while others seem condemned to failure. Let's look for a moment at the characteristics that mark one for success.

The first is discipline. Of course, at the heart of discipline is persistence. The great athlete, the successful business-man, the outstanding student all discipline themselves by conditioning and practice, committing themselves to long hours of physical and mental effort.

The second characteristic is determination. People who succeed work with a relentless determination. They allow nothing to deter them from their objectives. They will not be distracted.

The third characteristic for success is attention to detail. Nothing in their lives and career is too small or unimportant to demand their attention. Ray Kroc, of McDonald's fame, said, "Little things don't mean a lot, they mean everything."

We must
NEVER LOSE
the sense of
ADVENTURE,
that thirst for
KNOWLEDGE
or that
DETERMINATION
to explore the outer
limits of our own
ABILITIES.

—FORMER PRESIDENT
RONALD REAGAN

DON'T LIVE IN THE PAST

❧ ❧

The well-known Earl Nightingale commented in one of his presentations, "Don't water last year's crops." Peter Marshall, the late, great chaplain of the U.S. Senate, once wrote: "The years that are gone are graveyards into which all the persuasions of men have crumbled into dust." I think these two great men are, in their own ways, reminding us of a mode of living that is fraught with danger, with risk. They are saying

DON'T LIVE IN THE PAST.

You can neither change the past nor improve on it. Therefore, never live in the past, never dwell on the past. However, you can do something about today. You can change the future. Therefore, focus on today and tomorrow.

The great gift of life is time.
Use this time to learn something new, something positive each day. It will change our life and your world for the better. Remember, the future does not belong to the learned, it belongs to the learners.

The
YEARS THAT
are gone are
GRAVEYARDS
into which all the
PERSUASIONS
of men have
CRUMBLED
into dust.

—REV. PETER MARSHALL

THE POSSIBLE YOU

❧ ❧

Great men frequently focus on human potential because they observe people only minimally utilizing their abilities and resources. Shakespeare once said: "We know what we are, but know not what we may be."

More recently the late Dr. Norman Vincent Peale said: "Everybody has something greater in him than he ever knew." These two great men are focusing on human potential...
and I am here to tell you that human potential is limitless.
YOUR POTENTIAL IS LIMITLESS!!

THE POSSIBLE YOU resides somewhere among your untapped resources and little used skills!

While most people blunder through life with neither plans nor goals, let me urge you to put those same unused abilities to work becoming the possible you...
....committing yourself to one challenging project after the other
....acquiring the success that will give your life its greatest fulfillment.

Things that
MATTER MOST
must never be at the
MERCY OF
things that
MATTER LEAST.

—JOHANN GOETHE

THE DEFINITION OF SUCCESS

❧ ❧

Have you ever felt that you are spinning your wheels...
...that your life is going nowhere?
Perhaps the reason is that you haven't decided what direction your life should be taking. You haven't formulated YOUR definition of success.

Here is one man's definition of success:
> "SUCCESS IS THE CONTINUOUS JOURNEY TOWARDS THE ACHIEVEMENT OF PREDE-TERMINED, WORTHWHILE GOALS."

The implication of this definition of success is that you must carefully outline a set of goals that you want to achieve with your life.

Remember, success is not a destination. It is a continuing journey where you move from goal to goal, ever changing as you move from year to year in your life.

"Success is a personal standard..."
It means reaching for the highest that is in us...
...becoming all that we can be.
Success to each of us is choosing the goals that are important to us personally, then bending every effort to achieve them.

Everyone wants
to change
HUMANITY,
but nobody wants
TO CHANGE
himself.

—TOLSTOY

TAKE CONTROL OF YOUR LIFE

⚔ ⚕

Every person has a control center. That control center is one's mind. Further, the human mind has an enormous capacity for storing and evaluating information. Tragically, most people barely scratch the surface of this ability.

John Atkinson said, "If you don't run your own life, somebody else will." Therefore, if you want to take control of your life you must take charge of your control center. Never allow the wrong people and the wrong ideas to dominate that control center.

Permit me to suggest several steps that will not only enable you to take charge of your control center but also to maximize its enormous capacity:
Develop a mindset that says, "I will learn something new each day."
Always input powerful, positive ideas.
Constantly expose your mind to new and more creative ideas.
Never let hate or fear dominate your thoughts, for they will sap positive mental energy.

Base your life on principles that never change. This will give you a changeless core in a chaotically changing world. Finally, let your mind become completely dominated by this changeless Biblical principle:

"Whatsoever you would that men do unto you, do ye even so to them."

It must be
BORN IN MIND
that the tragedy of
LIFE DOESN'T
lie in not reaching
YOUR GOAL.
The tragedy lies
in having no
GOAL TO REACH.

—Dr. Benjamin E. Mays

ATTITUDE'S LIMITLESS POWER

❧ ❧

Brian Tracy once said that of all attributes necessary for success the one without which success is impossible is ATTITUDE. The more I live, the more I realize that the impact of attitude on my life is immeasurable. It is more important than skills, appearance, education, abilities, or money.

We cannot change the inevitable. However, we <u>can</u> change our attitude. Remember, attitude can make or break a business, a church, a company, a home, a club or any organization.

I am convinced that life is 10 percent what happens to me and 90 percent how I react to it. The lesson here is extremely important.
You are in charge of your attitudes.
You can be moody and depressed or happy and enthusiastic. The choice is yours.

Let me make this suggestion: Develop an attitude of optimisim...

...an attitude that says anything is possible.

Dr. Peale once said, "Any fact facing us is not as important as our attitude toward it. For that determines our success or failure."

People can't live
WITH CHANGE
if there is not a
CHANGELESS
core inside them.
THE KEY TO
the ability to change
is a changeless
SENSE OF WHO
you are, what you are
about and
WHAT YOU VALUE.

—STEPHEN R. COVEY

NEVER STOP LEARNING

❧ ❧

Dr. Nathan Pusey, a former president of Harvard University, said that if upon graduation we have taught the students to ask the right questions, we have succeeded. This says something important about commencement exercises, namely, learning does not stop here.

Perhaps real learning begins here!

One of the special attributes that sets apart

the ordinary from the extraordinary,

the winners from losers,

the successful from the "also rans,"

is their commitment to learning.

High achievers consciously focus on saturating themselves with information.

They continue to read,

to acquire knowledge involving a broad range of subjects.

They read voraciously,

from novels to newspapers

from biographies to books on business.

The lesson here is very important!

If you are looking for greater success in your chosen field...

If you wish to increase your interpersonal skills...

If you wish to enlarge the scope of your leadership abilities...

Then make this commitment:

"Each day I will learn something new."

And don't simply read...

...absorb, take notes, evaluate.

Remember,

"Wisdom is knowledge which has become a part of one's being."

You and I have a
RENDEZVOUS
with destiny. We can
PRESERVE FOR
our children this,
the last best
HOPE OF MAN
on earth, or we can
sentence them to take
THE FIRST STEP
into a thousand years
of darkness.

—Former President
Ronald Reagan

CHAMPIONS AND ALSO-RANS

✧ ✧

As I watched the Winter Olympics downhill skiing, I was reminded again of what a microscopic difference there is between the champion and the also-ran. The difference between the champion and the second, third or fourth is measured in hundredths of a second. The champion's name will hit the headlines and be remembered.

Second, third and fourth will be forgotten immediately.
There is a lesson here.
First, the difference between champions and also-rans is microscopic.
Second, to be a champion requires a bit more discipline...

...more effort

...more commitment!

Each of us wants to be a champion, a winner!
The difference between being number one and an also-ran requires increasing one's level of concentration...

...putting forth that extra effort that will provide victory.

It will mean knowing what you want and going for it with every fiber of your being. Napoleon Hill once said, "The one quality which one must possess to win is ... the knowledge of what one wants and a burning desire to possess it."

We live moment
BY MOMENT,
not year
BY YEAR.
Do the most
PRODUCTIVE
thing you can think of
with each
AND EVERY
moment as you live it,
and your future is
ASSURED.

—TOM HOPKINS

THE LAW OF USE OR LOSE

❧ ❧

Dennis Kimbro, in his outstanding book
Think And Grow Rich: A Black Choice,
which was based on Napoleon Hill's classic best seller,
uses the expression "use or lose." He points out that if you
do not make constant use of a talent, whether mental or
physical, you will lose it.

Ordinary people frequently look at famous celebrities in
sports or intellectual pursuits without realizing the enormous amount of practice and effort that went into their
success.

There is a vitally important lesson here for all of us. It is,
"Success in any field requires practice."
No great achievement is possible without constant practice! Use your mind, your intellect
    ...to increase your determination
    ...to expand your understanding
    ...to enlarge your mental commitment
...always remembering if I do not exercise my intellectual
abilities through intelligent practice they will atrophy as
surely as an unused arm or leg.

You are your
GREATEST ASSET.
Put your
TIME, EFFORT,
and money into
TRAINING,
grooming, and
ENCOURAGING
your greatest asset.

—TOM HOPKINS

THE DEFINITION OF LUCK

⋇ ⋇

I don't know about you, but I cannot count the number of times I have heard people say,

"Just look at him! He gets all the luck."

I've heard this statement made in reference to salesmen...

...in reference to businessmen...

...and in reference to professional people.

My conclusion after studying these so-called "lucky people" is that luck is never an accident. Lady luck never randomly taps one person on the shoulder and ignores the other. I have concluded that luck rarely just happens.

Luck is always created!

The question then is: "How can you create luck?" Well, one way to do it is

ALWAYS EXPECT THE BEST.

However, the best way to understand luck is to know this definition:

LUCK IS WHEN PREPARATION MEETS OPPORTUNITY.

Do you want to know how to make luck happen in your life? The answer is preparation . . . preparation for the opportunities that will inevitably come your way.

Happiness
is not a
DESTINATION;
it is a
METHOD
of life.

— Burton Hills

MAXIMIZE YOUR POWERS

❦ ❦

Have you ever noticed how people spend much of their lives making excuses for their faults? Many spend their lives justifying their faults. A well-known advertising man named Len Sumner said, "Some people spend their whole lives perfecting their faults."

The man who is looking for a life of success cannot dwell on his faults, but must maximize his strengths, his powers. Every person has talents he never really believes he has. You either develop these talents or you neglect them...
...and they erode through disuse.

To maximize your powers take the following steps.
Don't impose limitations on yourself!
Don't dwell on your failures!
Concentrate on your successes!
Then develop them!

While an old axiom says you can learn from your failures, you can also learn from your successes. Whenever you successfully accomplish something go over it REPEATED-LY until it is ingrained in your mind.
Then take steps to repeat that success!
Develop the optimism that says, "I can cope with every obstacle that life puts in my path."

The worst
BANKRUPT
in the world is
THE MAN
who has lost his
ENTHUSIASM.

—H.W. ARNOLD

PREPARATION

❧ ❧

A world-famous entertainer of years past was approached by a young aspiring performer who asked this question:

"How can I attain your level of success in this business?"

The famous performer reflected for a few moments and then replied with one word ... PREPARATION

Nothing is free. Some believe that creativity and inventiveness are the gifts of a few lucky people. This notion is totally false. Hard work, study and regular preparation is the only source of

great ideas...

...inventive solutions to problems and

...creative business strategies.

If you expect to be ready to seize that outstanding opportunity that will inevitably come your way, it will require PREPARATION.

And what does this preparation involve?

It requires study; daily, specific, thorough study.

It requires working intensely in your field to gain experience!

It requires complete focus of thought on the subject of your choice!

It requires filling your subconscious mind with material that will create success building ideas.

I am
ALWAYS READY
to learn, but I
DON'T ALWAYS
like being taught.

—WINSTON CHURCHILL

LIFE IN BALANCE

◈ ◈

There is a possibility that the success we strive for can turn to ashes in our hands, if our lives do not maintain the proper balance. So often we read about successful people who, upon achieving unusual heights, deteriorate rapidly because they fail to maintain balance in their lives.

One law of life is people need both work and play,
    ...both intellectual and physical exercise,
        ...both moments of quiet reflection and
           ...moments of intense activity.
           BALANCE IS THE KEY

Don't become too obsessed with your job...
    ...too obsessed with making money.
Don't become so consumed with a particular project that you neglect other areas necessary for a balanced life.

A Latin phrase says "Mens Sana in Corpore Sano" which means "A SOUND MIND IN A SOUND BODY." You will increase your ability to succeed if you make sure to establish time for thought and reflection...
    ...for recreation and exercise
        ...for family and friends.
           Remember, balance is the key!

...a society
CULTIVATES
whatever is
HONORED
there...

— PLATO

SUCCESSFUL LIFE

❧ ❧

How many of you would go bird hunting and discharge your gun into the sky in the vain hope that a bird might be flying by?

How many of you would enter the office of a travel agent and say, "I want to take a trip," and upon his saying "Where," you would reply "Anywhere is OK."

No such occurrence ever transpires! Hunting requires a target and travel demands a destination...
>AND A SUCCESSFUL LIFE REQUIRES
>CLEARLY DEFINED GOALS.

Put on paper a destination for your life. Then outline a detailed plan describing how you will get there. If you focus on an overriding goal for your life, you will find yourself automatically setting priorities that will enable you to reach your goal.

One of W. Clements Stone's 17 principles of success is
>DEFINITENESS OF PURPOSE.

To get where you want to go, he suggests, you must have a definite vision of your overall goal.

We live in a
TIME WHERE
not only anything we
CAN IMAGINE
seems possible,
but where the
POSSIBILITIES
range beyond what we
CAN IMAGINE.

—ALBERT ROSENFELD

THE POWER OF THOUGHT

⋈

Napoleon Hill wrote: "You have absolute control over but one thing, and that is your thoughts." Dennis Kimbro wrote: "You are the sum total of your thoughts."

The implications of these statements by these two brilliant authors is that what we think about is enormously important, for it will determine what we achieve and what we become!

While the brain is not a computer, it has certain computer-like qualities. When you decide to take some sort of action, it is almost like creating a program for that activity.

Put your mind to work on your goals. Program it day by day with whatever you're seeking to achieve.

Remember, the idea precedes the deed ...

... thoughts give birth to the actions!

Therefore, focus your thoughts on success,

abundance and positive goals.

Focus the enormous power of your thoughts on what you wish to accomplish.

Your deepest, most intense thoughts will in fact power you toward the level of achievement you demand of your life.

First, regardless
of age, education
OR PROFESSION
America's most
PRODUCTIVE
people share the
same set of basic skills.
Second, and
MOST IMPORTANT,
these skills are
LEARNABLE!

—DR. CHARLES GARFIELD

THE LAW OF EXPECTATION

❧ ❧

The world has a way of cooperating by conforming to our expectations. This is often referred to as the Law of Expectation. The Law of Expectation is this: "What you expect to happen usually will." Further, it means if you expect something, that expectation becomes a self-fulfilling prophecy.

The Law of Expectation works like this. If I say to myself as a salesperson, as I am approaching the office door of a business I am trying to sell, "These people aren't going to buy anything," chances are they won't. Conversely, if I am that same salesperson and approach that same office and say, "These people are definitely going to buy," chances are they will.

The Lesson: Put the Law of Expectation to work in your life to acquire YOUR desired results. Expect the best to happen. Always look for the best possible outcome.

Our individual world will respond to us in the way in which we see it. If our world sees us as happy, optimistic, enthusiastic people, that will become OUR self-fulfilling prophecy.

Peak performing
INDIVIDUALS
are at the core of any
EXCELLENT
organizations success.

—DR. CHARLES GARFIELD

THE SECRET OF SECURITY

❧ ❧

Have you noticed how many people are talking about job security today? They're obviously equating job security with financial or economic security. The news media has picked up the same theme.

They are looking for security in the wrong place. Listen to this statement by the brilliant author Stephen Covey: "Your economic security does not lie in your job. It lies in your own power to produce – to think, to learn, to create, to adapt. That's true financial independence. It is not having wealth; it's having the power to produce wealth."

Past history demonstrates that security does not lie in things; rather it lies within you. Therefore, if you are looking for security, develop your ability to think, study and learn. Focus your efforts on study and learning.

That is what security is all about.
It is developing one's talents to the level where they are able to produce the wealth that we desire. There is no other security.

Sometimes when
I CONSIDER
what tremendous
CONSEQUENCES
come from little
things ...I am tempted
TO THINK...
There are no
LITTLE THINGS.

—BRUCE BARTON

THE LAW OF THE HARVEST

❧ ❧

There is an old saying in corporate America that says, "You should be careful whom you step on, on the way up the corporate ladder. For they will be the ones who step on you, on your way down."

Perhaps this is just another way of stating,

THE LAW OF THE HARVEST
Which is:
We will always reap what we sow .....

.... No more, no less!

Sow kindness, caring and commitment, and that is what you will harvest. Sow hate, greed and selfishness and that is exactly what you will harvest.

The choice is yours!

Dag Hammarskjold, former general secretary of the United Nations, once said:

"You cannot play with the animal in you without becoming wholly animal, play with falsehood without forfeiting your right to truth,

play with cruelty without losing your sensitivity of mind.

He who wants to keep his garden tidy doesn't reserve a plot for weeds."

I know of no more
ENCOURAGING
fact than the
UNQUESTIONABLE
ability of man to
ELEVATE HIS
life by conscious
ENDEAVOR.

—HENRY DAVID THOREAU

DISCIPLINE

✄ ✄

There are many important keys to success. However, there are few more important than
SELF-DISCIPLINE.
We tend to think that people who succeed have a great deal of luck...
...that great opportunities keep coming their way. The truth is that this is probably never the case. Examine a very successful person and you will probably discover a very disciplined person.

People admire and envy those who are successful. However, they often fail to look at the enormous amount of hard work and discipline that make all of this success possible. These successful people discipline themselves, spending long hours of intense effort in preparation so that when opportunity arrives they are prepared to take advantage of it.

In a world where we are fun-oriented and entertainment-saturated, we need to remember that one of the keys to successful life is self-discipline. Discipline means working at getting better each day. And regardless of what you do for a living, if you work at getting better each day ...
SOMEDAY YOU WILL BE OUTSTANDING.

Knowledge is the
QUICKEST
and safest path
TO SUCCESS
in any area of life.

—CHARLES GIVENS

GOING THE EXTRA MILE

❧ ❧

Years ago the Creole shopkeepers in southern Louisiana had a word to describe that something extra they gave their customers. The word was "lagniappe," and it meant something extra. For example, if a customer asks for a dozen rolls, they might throw in a couple of extra. That was "lagniappe."

This old custom might well be applied today in the form of GOING THE EXTRA MILE in everything that we do. Elbert Hubbard, the essayist, wrote, "Folks who never do anymore than they get paid for, never get paid for anymore than they do."

In an age of self-gratification where you give only what you get paid for, going the extra mile can be a very important strategy if we are looking for greater success. The reason for this is that those who go the extra mile stand out in our society. They stand out because they are willing to give before they receive.

Going the extra mile will bring outstanding results. Since there is no traffic jam on the extra mile your extra efforts will be recognized in the business arena as an important value-added bonus.

If you give more than is asked, you will reap great rewards. The idea simply reinforces a proven Biblical principle: "Give and it shall be given unto you."

No one
HAS EVER
been known
TO ACHIEVE
permanent success
WITHOUT DOING
more than he was
PAID FOR.

—NAPOLEON HILL

ACHIEVEMENT OR PRAISE

❧ ❧

Ask yourself this question: "What am I working for?"
>   Am I working for money?
>>   ...or for achievement?
>>>   ...or am I working for praise?

Many people when asked why they work will immediately reply that they are working for money. This is a short-sighted attitude! There are others who work for praise,
>   for a pat on the back,
>>   for recognition.

Those who achieve outstanding success, however, are those who work for achievement, for accomplishment. For when you work for accomplishment you discover that money is the by product. Those who work for money will never feel the satisfaction of accomplishing great goals. Those who work for achievement will find that with it comes the money they need.

There is a plaque on the wall in the lobby of the Coca-Cola building in downtown Altanta with this inscription:
>   "There is no limit to what a man can do or where
>   he can go if he doesn't mind who gets the credit."

This is what we all need to learn. Don't worry about that pat on the back. Don't worry about the money. It will come, if we work for achievement and accomplishment of goals.

The habit of going the
EXTRA MILE...
gives one the
ONLY LOGICAL
reason for asking
FOR INCREASED
compensation.

—NAPOLEON HILL

WINNING STRATEGIES

❧ ❦

Let me share with you today my personal
WINNING STRATEGIES

First, I always attempt to expand my sphere of influence. This is done by never refusing to help someone who asks for assistance. If it is at all possible, I attempt to do a favor for anyone who asks.

The second strategy is this: I try to absorb as much knowledge as I possibly can about the business I am in, so that I am able to give the best possible service and advice available.

Finally, I always try to put first things first. This means I need to evaluate what is important or critical and put that at the top of the list of duties that I must perform on any given day. Too often we get caught up in activities that are fruitless, postponing what should have top priority in our lives.

Goethe said, "Things which MATTER MOST must never be at the mercy of things which matter least."

These three steps are my way of making my life more successful. Perhaps they will also help you.

Today's world takes no pity on the person who GETS LAZY about learning. EITHER YOU TAKE personal responsibility for continuing your EDUCATION, or you end up without the knowledge you need to protect YOUR CAREER.

—PRICE PRITCHETT

DEMAND YOUR BEST

❧ ❧

The reason people accept mediocre performance is because they do not demand the best from themselves. How many times have you heard people say,

"I can't remember names" or

"I can't spell," or

"I'm not good at numbers."

We each have a decision to make. That decision involves the question, "What do I want to be good at?"

Your job, for example,

Do you want to be the best you can be at your job?

What it boils down to is this: You can be good at almost anything you choose! It all revolves around whether you are going to DEMAND THE BEST from yourself.

Successful people demand the best from themselves. They do not settle for second best! They focus their abilities on the accomplishment of their goals. They have a will to win. However, they know the will to win means nothing, if there is no will to prepare.

Make your decision now. Decide now to mobilize your intellect and skills, demanding the best from them ...

... so you can achieve the successes that are your fondest dreams.

You need to know that
RESISTANCE TO
change is always a
DEAD END
street.

—PRICE PRITCHETT

THE RESOUCE OF TIME

✠ ✠

In recent years there have been a number of companies specializing in time management. Perhaps this is because it is, first of all, our number one basic resource and, second of all, most people squander or waste a great deal of time.

While it is true that the great gifts of intellect and ability are very important, the time necessary to develop them and use them is critical. The bottom line is this: Your basic resource is time. Careful planning for its use is essential to success.

Here are some suggestions:

Divide your available time each day into very carefully defined areas. For example after your days work, set aside time for wife and family,

      for study and intellectual pursuits,

         and for personal recreation.

Note the meaning of the word recreation. It means re-create. This important time is vital because it enables you to recreate your being, your mind, your soul!

Make this promise to yourself:
"I will plan each day, setting aside time for study, rest and intellectual pursuits. I will not squander my time, but will invest it intelligently."

In today's world,
CAREER SUCCESS
belongs to the
COMMITTED...
To those who work from
THE HEART...
Who invest themselves
PASSIONATELY
in their goals...and who
recommit quickly when
change reshapes
THEIR WORK.

—PRICE PRITCHETT

THE IMPORTANCE OF SELF IMAGE

❧ ❦

One of the great problems we all have is the excess emotional baggage we carry with us from when we were growing up. For example, the first words that most of us learn all seem to be negative, such as:

... No

... Don't do that

... You can't do that

We are not only conditioned by these do's and don'ts of childhood but this conditioning usually creates in us an inadequate self image.

The reason this is so important is because your self image is the giant controller of your personal destiny. Your image of yourself will determine the direction of your life.

To deal with the negatives of childhood you must develop an image of yourself as a winner ...

... as a contributor

... as an achiever

... as a believer in yourself.

The only way for you to overcome these negatives and create a powerful, positive self image and overcome the negatives heaped on you while growing up is by formulating a series of positive, personal declarations to be repeated and visualized every day of your life. Some of them are as follows:

I believe in myself. I am not afraid of failure. I am a winner.

Add more to that short list and use them daily to build a self image that will power you to your greatest success.

Experience is not
WHAT HAPPENS
to a man. It is what
MAN DOES
with what
HAPPENS TO HIM.

—ALDOUS HUXLEY

IMAGINATION

✧ ✦

Every project begins in your imagination as an idea. Your ability to think, to dream, to imagine is

WHERE SUCCESS BEGINS

... and every person has the ability to use his imagination to create ideas.

Well, then, where do YOU begin? The answer is, look around you to seek out the type of career you would like, or focus on the business you would like to be in ... then imagine yourself in that position.

What is required more than anything else is the ability to dream. Woodrow Wilson said it best: "We grow great by dreams. All big men are dreamers." All men who have achieved great things have been dreamers. See yourself doing the things you will be doing when you've reached your goals. Your imagination will enable you to see the end results of your efforts before they actually occur.

Do you want power?

Do you want leadership?

Do you want wealth?

Then set your sights on your goals and put your imagination to work.

To acquire ideas and act on them will be the result of taking Joe Karbo's advise. He called it RSVP ... read, study, visualize, perform. Remember, RSVP.

Failure? I never
ENCOUNTERED IT.
All I ever met were
TEMPORARY
setbacks.

—DOTTIE WALTERS

THE PRICE OF SUCCESS

I do not like lotteries. My reasoning is that they perpetuate one of the most damaging beliefs ever conceived by the mind of man. That is

"It is possible to get something for nothing".

This is untrue because it runs contrary to a basic law of life, namely, the law of cause and effect. Dennis Kimbro stated it beautifully: "At the counter of success there are no bargains. A price must always be paid in advance, and in full."

What then is THE PRICE OF SUCCESS
I see it as a four step process:
First, you need to make the choice.
Second, you need to have the desire.
Third, translate your desires into ideas.
Finally, translate your ideas into action.

On Sunday, April 5, 1992, America's greatest entrepreneur died. He did not come from an Ivy League college. He did not get his ideas from the canyons of Wall Street. He entered this world in the dust bowls of Oklahoma, was raised in a small Missouri town and began his business in an even less pretentious village in Arkansas. This great man who committed himself to prodigious amounts of hard work was Sam Walton.

Guess what were the two basic principles of America's most successful entrepreneur? I will tell you. Burn them into your mind: HONESTY AND HARD WORK.

Passionate people
EMBRACE
what they love and
NEVER GIVE UP!

—DANIELLE KENNEDY

THE MIND

❈ ❧

There is one part of your physical person that is never at rest. It doesn't matter whether you are asleep, unconscious, or fully awake, your mind is never at rest. It is always functioning, always thinking, always occupied with an idea.

Let me offer you a suggestion on how you can take advantage of this amazing phenomenon. First, remember that the conscious mind feeds information to the subconscious mind. Therefore, to make use of the subconscious mind while you are asleep you can feed that subconscious mind all of your carefully prepared goals ....

      ... all of your positive declarations

        ... all of your fondest desires.

Avoid focusing on negative thoughts. For what happens is that while we are asleep our subconscious mind will remain focused on all of these negatives. This can have an enormous effect on our outlook when we are awake.

Awake or asleep, your mind is a powerful engine. When alert and wide awake, you have control over what enters that mind. When asleep, we are most vulnerable.

Something I find extremely effective is reading over my goals as a last exercise just before falling asleep each night. They will become increasingly vivid and real because your subconscious mind will be absorbing them all night long, delivering them to you in the morning with a clarity that will add enormous conviction and power.

The hand
THAT ROCKS
the cradle, rules
THE WORLD.

—OLD SPANISH PROVERB

FAILURE OR SUCCESS

◅ ▻

We are always talking about the price of success:
...The commitment that must be made
   ...The hard work that needs to be invested
      ...The desire that needs constant cultivation.
All in all, success doesn't just happen. It is usually the result
of years and years of hard work and unrelenting effort.

Now if you think success is costly, let's take a look at failure.
Nothing in this life is more costly than failure.
Nothing has more impact on our society than the failed
lives of those who have lost hope.

Walk the downtown streets of any of our major cities and
you will see the high cost of failure to our society and
country. Look at the faces. You will see
...no hope
   ...no joy
      ...no excitement
...only people who have given up on themselves whose
pride and self respect is gone. How much untapped talent
and unused skill have atrophied in the streets of our great
cities. This is why failure is so costly. It enslaves, then
destroys men's lives.

The lesson: Pay the price of success. Commit to using all
of your abilities to achieve your cherished goals. It will
be your greatest value.

Let the wise
LISTEN
and add to their
LEARNING,
and let the discerning
GET GUIDANCE.

—THE BIBLE

ENTHUSIASM

⊰ ⊱

To understand people one must understand that we are ruled more by emotion than by logic. When people make a buying decision though they may sound like they have come to a very logical conclusion, the decision is probably being made on an emotional level.

For that reason, people are moved and inspired by other people who are happy and vibrant. People love other people who are enthusiastic ... enthusiastic about life, about their jobs, about their families, about their relationships.

It is interesting to look at the derivation of the word "enthusiasm." The core word comes from two Greek words "en theos," which means possessed by God. The first meaning of the word enthusiasm is "being possessed by a supernatural inspiration."

There are so many people today who are so jaded and bored they can't get excited about anything. Let me urge you to secure a line of work or a position that you can enjoy, that you can get enthusiastic about, remembering that if you want to influence people positively, nothing is more powerful than enthusiasm. No one can resist happy, optimistic, enthusiastic people. These are the people who make things happen, changing our world into a better place to live.

Little things
DON'T MEAN
a lot, they mean
EVERYTHING.

—RAY KROC

PERSISTENCE

꙳ ꙳

Truly, one of the most important characteristics of success is
PERSISTENCE
... a "never-give-up" attitude.
The world of tennis was transfixed and inspired by the never give up attitude of Jimmy Connors in his epic battles on the tennis court. In my mind, he is the quintessential never-give-up example for all of us.

The reason millions were riveted to their TV sets during Jimmy's run for the US Open Championship in 1991 is because people intensely dislike the quitter, but adore the person who will never give up. They identify with him. They visualize themselves as being like him.
Jimmy Connors is our number one example of relentless persistence.

For those of you who are in sales, remember this fact:
Sixty percent of all buyers say "no" four times before they say "yes."
Lesson: Don't quit after the first "no."
Another fact: It takes an average of 5.5 visits to a potential buyers office to close a sale.
Lesson: Don't quit after the first visit.

Some have spent half their lives developing an idea and then quit just before it was about to become a success. There is an old saying that we would all do well to remember: "Quitters never win and winners never quit."

If you can
    DREAM IT,
you can
DO IT.

—Walt Disney

SELF-CONFIDENCE

❧ ❧

People who fail usually lack confidence. If you lack confidence in yourself and your abilities you will rarely if ever succeed. This indicates the
IMPORTANCE OF SELF-CONFIDENCE

People like to be involved with people who have confidence in themselves. Bosses give important tasks to people who they feel have the confidence in themselves to get the job done. Companies hire, trust, depend on, believe in people who have confidence.

Self-confidence is a result of self-knowledge, so the first step in developing self-confidence is determining what you are good at, where your strengths lie ... and making every effort to develop these strengths through study and learning. The more effective you are in the use of your strengths, the more self-confident you become. The more confidence you have in yourself, the more effective you will become in your position. Self-confidence grows as we focus wholeheartedly on mobilizing our capabilities and skills. This is what enables us to plan and act consistently ...

... to get results

... to manage change to achieve superior success.

Continue to build your self-confidence by accomplishing small goals thus proving to yourself that you ARE a winner. As your confidence grows, accept even greater challenges until you KNOW you are a winner and are capable of overcoming the small setbacks that are a part of life.

People who say
IT CANNOT
be done should
NOT INTERRUPT
those who are
DOING IT.

— Unknown

RISKS OF SELF-LIMITING BELIEFS

∗ ∗

When Napoleon Hill wrote:
"Whatever a man can conceive and believe, he can achieve,"
he must have thought about the terrible limitations people place on themselves by their self-limiting beliefs. The most tragic examples of this are to be seen in third world countries. In these countries there are many tragic beliefs that have imprisoned millions of people in lives of poverty and disease.

A man's beliefs become his realities. When Columbus sailed for the new world, many believed he would sail off the end of the earth into oblivion. Now that is a self-limiting belief! Even to this day people deify animals and worship snakes. Can you see how these twisted beliefs distort a man's outlook?

You must believe that there is no limit to what you can achieve if you mobilize all your skills and talents. Then practice and study to sharpen those skills. You must believe that you have the ability to get what you want in life. All it requires, is for you to develop these skills.

Always remember, as I have said before, your beliefs are your realities and they will either limit or expand your horizon.
If you believe you can overcome great obstacles ...
         ... achieve great goals
                  ...accomplish outstanding successes,
then develop your skills in that direction.
There will be no limit to what you can do.
You will discover a life of satisfaction and fulfillment.

We are drowning in
INFORMATION
and starved for
KNOWLEDGE.

—JOHN NAISBITT

THE VALUE OF GOALS

❧ ❧

I love Harvey Mackey's statement, "If you don't have a destination, you will never get there." What he is talking about here are goals as the secret to achievement. Goals are the blueprint for life that each person needs to clearly define.

The first step to getting to the destination of your choice is setting goals. This does not mean they should be vague wishes or dreams that you keep in your head. These important steps in your life must be put on paper in explicit detail. For without goals your life will be aimless and unfocused.

The second step is knowing what you want. Most people have no idea where they are going. Once you know what you want and have set your goals, then you can focus all your study, practice and effort on accomplishing them.

For example, is one of your goals the desire to own and operate your own company? If so, it is not going to happen by just dreaming about it. It will require spending enormous amounts of time developing your understanding and skills in that business.

Do not procrastinate!
Make your decision now!
Begin putting your goals on paper today ...
... remembering this statement by one of the first great motivators,

> "The world has the habit of making room for the man whose words and actions show that he knows where he is going."

Individual
RESPONSIBILITY,
however, stresses the
present; each
INDIVIDUAL IS
responsible for
EVERYTHING
he or she does.

—JOHN NAISBITT

THINK

_{❧ ❧}

Many important business leaders believe that the toughest task that they perform is to think. If this seems strange to you, let me point out something. The most imitated company in the country, if not the world, is IBM. What do you think the motto of this great company is? I will tell you. It is one word.

THINK

Thinking is the source of all creativity and vision. The focus of what I have to say is that if we want to come up with new and unusual ideas for business and government we must set aside time to think without interruption, shutting out the noise and chaos of the city.

My son saw an old movie of Mr. Tom Watson Sr., IBM's visionary leader, giving a presentation to a group of his employees. Across the front of the podium was written in huge letters one word, "THINK." This is obviously why IBM became the number one trend setter in computers and software.

Recently, a fax was sent to my office that has this very interesting quote: "There are two ways to slide easily through life: to believe everything or to doubt everything; both ways save us from thinking."

I guess my point today is this: "Big thinking precedes big achievement." You have to think big to be big.
Visionary thinking is always the source of great ideas. The Bible has something very important to say about it: "Where there is no vision the people perish."

The new
RESPONSIBILITY
of society is to reward
THE INITIATIVE
of the
INDIVIDUAL.

—JOHN NAISBITT

THE POWER OF REPETITION

❦ ❦

One of the more important strategies for success is to deal with habits that condemn us to failure before we even get started.

For example, a young friend of mine said emphatically that he doesn't like people. What he doesn't realize when he says this is that he doesn't like himself.

To deal with habits and ideas that create obstacles to successful life we need to create positive, success-building ideas and repeat them to ourselves daily.
Repetition is the key.
This will etch them into your mind.
There is enormous power in this process ...
　　　... and I can guarantee outstanding results.

Repeat these declarations and measure the result:
　　I like myself and other people.
　　　　After careful research I am very decisive.
　　　　　I possess an abundant supply of energy.
　　　　　　I always remember names.
　　　　　　I can bring enormous concentration
　　　　　　to bare on any subject.
　　　　　　I am an achiever.
Remember, repetition is the key.
REPTITION WILL MAKE IT HAPPEN.

Consistently high
PERFORMANCE
comes from
A BALANCE
of work
AND LEISURE.

—DALE CARNEGIE

CONTROL YOUR DESTINY

❧ ❧

One of the unfortunate characteristics of many people in today's society seems to be a penchant for blaming some-one else or some vague environmental condition of one kind or another for their failures. Statements like

> ... "I couldn't help it"
> ... "I didn't know what I was doing"
> ... "I didn't get a chance"

are commonly heard from those who refuse to accept responsibility.

These questions here are extremely important, namely,

> Am I responsible for what I do? And
> ... Am I responsible for my success or failure?

The answer to both questions is a resounding YES.
Unless you take complete control of your life and career, and assume full responsibility for yourself, it is a good bet that no one else will.

My advice is:

> ... look at yourself
> ... assess your skills and abilities

then commit yourself to the challenge of learning and studying to develop these abilities, putting them to use in securing the life you want.

You can be what you want to be! There are no excuses! Make your commitment now to take full responsibility for your life, then develop all of those unused talents, dedi-cating them to a life of positive fulfillment.

The time to repair
THE ROOF
is when
THE SUN
is shining.

—JOHN F. KENNEDY

FOCUS ON THE DESTINATION

❧ ❦

Where do you want to go with your life? What kind of career would you really like to have? Do you have a dream,
   ... a longing,
      ... hope that remains unrealized?

There have been many both past and present who have achieved outstanding success in spite of insuperable obstacles.

One such person was a boy from Kansas whose legs were terribly burned in an accident, ostensibly condemning him to life as a cripple. This boy grew up to be one of the world's outstanding runners. In fact, in an unregistered time trial with no press present it is said he broke the four-minute barrier for the mile ... this he accomplished a half generation before Roger Bannister's highly publicized sub-four minute mile. For your information this boy was Glen Cunningham.

Focus on your destination. Etch it in your mind. Decide whether it is worth your effort, whether it has an overriding importance in your life. If that destination is too big to be denied, then commit yourself to the effort and time required to achieve it ...
regardless of the obstacles,
    regardless of the barriers,
        you can make that dream come true.

You cannot
always control
CIRCUMSTANCES,
but you
CAN CONTROL
your own
THOUGHTS.

—C.E. POPPLESTONE

DO WHAT YOU LOVE

❧ ❧

Dr. Jim Lundy has written a book entitled *Lead, Follow, or Get Out of the Way*. In it he makes this observation:
"A stress expert claims that most people in our country don't like their work. (And most don't like their spouses, which means, apparently, that most of us neither want to go to work nor want to go home!)"

Seek out a career or a job that you love, remembering Dr. Marsha Sinetar's statement: "Do what you love, the money will follow." Than, make a commitment to being the best that you can be in that career. Understand that in a career of your choice what you do matters.

If you are able to find a career that you love, if you restlessly search until you do find that career, I am sure you will begin to look forward to Monday instead of Friday, and will find satisfaction and fulfillment in your job.

The men who try to
DO SOMETHING
and fail are infinitely
BETTER THAN
those who try to
DO NOTHING
and succeed.

—LLOYD JONES

LIFE'S GREAT TRAGEDY

❦ ❧

Have you ever noticed that in our educational system virtually no one offers a class on "HOW TO PLAN YOUR LIFE." It all seems so obvious that this very activity is the secret to achieving the successes in life that you want.

It is such a simple process. Look around you. Look at your abilities. Decide what you want to do and write it on paper in the form of daily, weekly and monthly goals. As each goal is achieved, you add new goals. Now, why don't more people do this? Why don't more people work toward specific achievement?

My opinion: This is LIFE'S GREAT TRAGEDY. It is the fact that goals are not achieved. It is the fact that goals are not even made. I found this quote in Dr. Kimbro's book *Think and Grow Rich: A Black Choice*. It is by Dr. Benjamin E. Mays, president emeritus of Morehouse College in Atlanta:

> "It must be born in mind that the tragedy of life doesn't lie in not reaching your goal. The tragedy lies in having no goal to reach."

Structure your plan for life.

Put your goals on paper.

Read them daily and

> I will guarantee you it will transform your life into a life of achievement.

Every failure
IS A STEP
to success.

—WILLIAM WHEWELL

PERSONAL PRODUCTIVITY

❧ ❧

Have you ever wondered why certain people are so enormously productive? There could be a number of reasons for this. It could be that they are
... more focused,
    ... more goal oriented, or
        ... they work for specific achievement.
            ... Maybe they just put in long hours of
            hard work and effort.
While all of the above is extremely important, perhaps the sine qua non of personal productivity is embodied in a single factor. The most productive people in the world tend to be students all their lives.

The great risk of life is the problem of intellectual stagnation. The challenge of life is to develop the productivity that brings the positive rewards we are all looking for
... better jobs
    ... better homes and
        ... better living conditions.

Make a serious commitment to becoming a perpetual student, always open to new ideas, new opportunities and new ventures. I can guarantee you that the result will be a dramatic change in your life, transforming you from a member of the pack to a leader of the pack.

I am not
DISCOURAGED,
because every
wrong attept
DISCARDED
is another step
FORWARD.

—Thomas Edison

CHANGING THE WORLD

❧ ❧

Most of us look out at the world sadly and say that there are a lot of changes for the better that need to be made. No one would deny this. Changing the world for the better is not something that will come easily. Most of us view the vast changes that are necessary and wonder, "Where can we begin to affect any kind of positive change."

It appears to me that there are two important concepts to remember when talking about the world and what it needs. First of all, one needs to remember, as John Donne said, "No man is an island unto himself." Every human being is inseparably linked to every other human being by the common bond of humanity. If one man hurts, we all hurt.

The other observation that we need to remember is a statement made by the great Russian author Tolstoy who said,
> "Everyone wants to change humanity, but nobody want to change himself."

You can make a difference in the world in which you live. You can be the candle that dispels the darkness around you. Your first step in making your home, your community, your town, your city a better place in which to live is to become the best that you can be in whatever you do, remembering that your willingness to change for the better is what will make your world a better place in which to live.

You can be
DISCOURAGED
by failure – or you can
learn from it. So
GO AHEAD
and make mistakes.
Make all you can.
BECAUSE,
remember, that's where
you'll find success,
on the far side of
FAILURE.

—Thomas J. Watson

MAXIMIZE YOUR POTENTIAL

❧ ❧

I keep coming back to the subject of the importance of human potential. It is my observation that achievement of one's potential is directly related to one's ability to know what one wants. It is also directly related to one's desire.

It is obviously important for each of us to determine exactly what it is that we want
    ... in our careers
        ... in our personal lives and
            ... in all of our activities.

Once we understand what we want, then we can begin to cultivate the desire to acquire it. Therefore, the first step in maximizing your potential is having a desire to achieve your goals. It is also axiomatic that you can usually get what you want if you want it hard enough. A burning and irrepressible desire for something will usually drive a man to its achievement. So, the steps in maximizing one's personal potential are as follows:

1. Know what you want.
2. Cultivate a burning desire to achieve what you want.
3. Develop and sharpen all the skills and unused powers to achieve the goal that you have in mind.
4. Finally, take inventory of your skills and abilities and focus them on the achievement of the dreams that are your heart's desire.

I can guarantee you that this procedure will result in reaching goals that you never thought were possible.

You can do
WHAT YOU
want to do.
YOU CAN
be what you
WANT TO BE.

—R. David Thomas

THE POWER OF PERSISTENCE

❧ ❧

One of the lessons of life is that in order to succeed at achieving our goals it will be necessary to overcome adversity. It will be necessary to overcome obstacles that appear to be insuperable.

The reason that it is so important to be a goal-oriented person is because goal-oriented people are unusually persistent. They do not know the word quit. One of the more recent U.S. Presidents made this observation: "A man is not finished when he is defeated; he is finished when he quits." The accomplishment of every worthwhile goal requires persistence ...

... persistence in the face of obstacles,

... persistence in the face of what appears to be insuperable problems.

Persistence is an attitude that says, "I will never give up until I have reached my goal."

Two important facts must be remembered at all times. The first is, "the odds are always with us if we keep on trying." The second is a statement made by another wise man who said, "There is only one way you can fail – and that's to quit." Success may not require a great amount of knowledge about anything, but it does call for relentless persistence in the use of all your unused talents.

The one thing
OVER WHICH
you have absolute
CONTROL IS
your own thoughts.
IT IS THIS
that puts you in a
POSITION
to control your
OWN DESTINY.

—PAUL C. THOMAS

THE POWER OF VISUALIZATION

✦ ✦

A fact that I didn't realize was so important in my life is that I have always had a vision or a picture in my mind of what I wanted. It was not until much later in my life that I discovered the importance also of putting my goals on paper and then visualizing them.

One of the great, inspiring aspects of reading is that your mind will cooperate by creating a picture of the scenes and descriptions of what you are reading in a book. This natural creative ability possessed by all people can be put to work on a daily basis to help achieve your highest hopes,
         ... your fondest dreams
              ... your noblest ambitions.

Follow this procedure:
Write your goals out in detail, in the present tense.
Then, visualize yourself already in possession of them.
Follow this procedure several times each day and you will suddenly discover that the mental picture has become a reality.

It works like this:
Act sad and you will become sad.
Act happy and you will become happy. You will become the way you act.

Perhaps Winston Churchill understood this when he said, "The empires of the future are the empires of the mind."

Forget about the
CONSEQUENCES
of failure.
FAILURE IS
only a temporary
change in
DIRECTION TO
set you straight for your
NEXT SUCCESSES.

—DENIS E. WAITLEY

WORRY

I wonder if all of you who are reading to these words realize the debilitating effect of worry. Worry not only affects us emotionally but affects us physically, at times rendering us incapable of functioning at any level, much less at our highest possible level of efficiency.

Many years ago, one of my mentor's observed, "Most of the things we worry about never happen." This is a thought that has helped me immeasurably over the years.

There are two steps that can be taken to deal with the problem of worry.
First, develop your skills, talents and abilities!
Highly developed talents will always translate into greater confidence ...
... and confidence defeats worry. Confidence says,

> "I can cope with every problem that comes my way.
> I can overcome every obstacle.
> I can achieve success in the face of any difficulty."

Second, focus this confidence on every worry,
                    ... every anxiety,
for confidence born of preparation will always enable you
to rise above the worries that would destroy you.

The person
INTERESTED IN
success has to
LEARN TO VIEW
failure as a healthy,
INEVITABLE PART
of the process of
GETTING TO
the top.

—DR. JOYCE BROTHERS

POSSIBILITY THINKING

❧ ❧

I keep thinking how important it is for all of us to get the most out of our lives. By the most I mean the most happiness, abundance, comfort, and excitement. It is apparent that most people do not get the most out of their lives. The reason: They do not subject themselves to POSSIBILITY THINKING.

David Robinson, the great professional basketball player and graduate of the Naval Academy, was once interviewed on 60 Minutes. He has in a sense adopted 97 children from all walks of life. He meets with them regularly and tells them all the time, "You can be anything you want to be."

No one in the world limits you except yourself. On the Avenue of Americas in New York City is a marvelous building once owned by the J.C. Penny Company. The slogan over the door says: "The only limits to our future are those we impose on ourselves."

What would you like to be? You have the answer. It exists right in your own mind ... a mind that contains all the ideas and ability necessary to achieve your highest ambitions. Possibility thinking requires systematic prospecting of your mind.

Remove the self-defeating thoughts from your mind. Replace them with Winston Churchill's words: "Never, never, never, give in." That is possibility thinking.

Successful people
ARE NOT AFRAID
to fail.
THEY ACCEPT
their failures and
CONTINUE ON.

—Unknown

MORE ON PERSERVERANCE

❧ ❧

There is a popular saying that goes: "When the going gets tough the tough get going." This focuses again on the subject of persistence, something we have talked about before.

One of the realities of life is that we will inevitably be faced with problems, obstacles. Some of these obstacles are created by our own failure. To overcome, therefore, will require persistence. John D. Rockefeller said, "I do not think there is any other quality so essential to success of any kind as the quality of perseverance. It overcomes almost everything, even nature." The man who achieves great things, who is blessed with superior accomplishments is the man who when knocked to the canvas gets up again and works with relentless persistence toward his goal.

One of the leading American businessmen made this perceptive statement about success. His name is H. Ross Perot and he said, "Most people give up just when they are about to achieve success. They quit on the one-yard line. They give up at the last minute of the game, one foot from a winning touchdown."

The message is clear: PERSISTENCE, PERSISTENCE, PERSISTENCE.
We will never be defeated if we never quit!!

Expect the best
and it
WILL HAPPEN.
Expecting the best
MORE OFTEN
than not becomes a
SELF-FULFILLING
prophecy.

—W.A.

BORN TO WIN

❧ ❧

I find it very interesting that few people feel they have been born to win! Perhaps this is why so many people are condemned to failure before they even start their careers.

The point which is important for you to understand about this message is that your belief in your ability to succeed will enhance dramatically your actual success. Or as one author put it so clearly in his most recent book: "Believe in yourself when no one else does."

The secret to success is specific achievement. It requires focusing on specific goals that can and will be accomplished by effort and commitment and, strangely, the more we accomplish the more we realize the opportunity for growth and accomplishment. Again, all of us need to remember to say to ourselves, "We can do any task." When we say this to ourselves, we will receive the empowerment to do so.

Behind all success then is commitment. The two core ingredients of commitment are faithfulness and persistence. The third ingredient that gives life to the first two is action. Each of us has the ability and talent to change our individual world. Find your purpose. Search for that compelling vision. Then make your commitment and you will find that you too can be a leader ...

you too can make a positive difference!

The success
COMBINATION
in business is:
DO WHAT
you do better ... and
DO MORE
of what you do.

—D.J. SCHWARTZ

STRATEGIES FOR SUCCESS

❧ ❧

Let me share with you today some important steps that are essential strategies for success. The first step toward success is to establish clearly defined goals that you want to achieve. These goals then need to be redefined on a regular basis as certain of them are accomplished and new ones are established. Without clearly defined goals and a commitment to achieve them, success will not be possible.

A second strategy that is critical to success is shaping goals involving important achievement that not only make a difference in your life but in the lives of others. In other words, every person needs to know that what he does matters. Important goals lead us in that direction. They are critical strategies for success. For people are productive to the degree that they believe that what they do matters in the world in which they live.

A third strategy for success lies in the ability to mobilize all your talents – intellectual, physical, mental and psychological – focusing them on the specific achievement to which you are committed. It is as you unlock your ability to excel by mobilizing all these resources that you are able to reach the level of success that you seek.

Zig Ziglar was right when he said, "Success is the maximum utilization of the ability that you have."

The possible you,
RESIDES
somewhere between
YOUR UNTAPPED
resources and little
USED SKILLS.

— W.A.

DEALING WITH NEGATIVES

＊ ＊

One of the most self-defeating attitudes we need to deal with on a daily basis is negative thinking. Negativism is so dangerous because it says, "I can't win this contract. I can't do this job. If I get this job I won't know how to do it. I won't be able to learn how to do it." Thousands fail because of the virus of negativism.

There are two steps that need to be taken to deal with this self-defeating attitude. The first step is: Associate with positive people. Develop in-depth associations only with those people who are upbeat, positive and enthusiastic about the future and about your possibilities.

The second step: You must disassociate yourself as rapidly as possible from any negative thinking and negative thinking people. You cannot permit these people to infect you with this deadly virus, making a cess pool out of your mind.

You must constantly give yourself these positive affirmations:
"My possibilities are limitless. I have all the ability necessary to survive successfully in this highly competitive world."

Let these words embody your reaction to every negative attack:
"Positive thinking is reacting positively to every negative situation."

Wisdom is
KNOWLEDGE
which has
BECOME A
part of one's
BEING.

—Unknown

KEYS TO GREATER PRODUCTIVITY

How would you like to be in the top 1 percent of the successful people in this world? Here are three steps you can take that will elevate you to this level. These steps are outlined in Tom Hopkins excellent book entitled *The Official Guide to Success*.

The first key to greater productivity: Write down on a piece of paper each evening the six most important tasks that you need to do the next day. This appears to be very simple, however, most people do not succeed in accomplishing even one of the most important tasks they need to do each day because they are confused and buried under minor trivialities that have taken on major importance in their lives.

The second step: Rank these six items in order of importance, from the hardest first, down to the easiest last. When you have done this, you can put this list away until the following day because you know you have already prioritized your whole world of activity for the next day. If you only finish one single thing you can do each day, that one item will put you far ahead of the pack because most people never get their most important task done on any given day.

The third key: Review the past day's list. Then place the unfinished tasks at the head of the next day's list. If achievement is your goal, these three steps will generate superior achievement.

You are the
SUM TOTAL
of your
THOUGHTS.

—Dennis Kimbro

LEARNING CREATES ENTHUSIASM

❧ ❧

All of those who talk about motivation ultimately focus on the importance of enthusiasm. Enthusiasm is so important!! Enthusiasm motivates us and other people more than anything else. Enthusiasm is much more persuasive than logic if we are trying to lead someone to our point of view.

The important question is: "How do I maintain a high level of enthusiasm?" The secret is learning! Remember how excited you were when you learned how to read or how to count or how to ride a bicycle? Learning new concepts has a way of re-energizing our enthusiasm.

Perhaps this is why so many wise people recommend that we become dedicated learners throughout our lives. An old saying that has always troubled me is: "You can't teach an old dog new tricks." The implication is that there is a point at which one cannot learn something new. The truth is, we must never stop learning!! The truth is, we can always learn regardless of our age and regardless of our position in life.

To maintain a high level of enthusiasm, life must always be a restless search for new knowledge.

Folks who never do
ANY MORE
than they get
PAID FOR,
never get paid for
ANYMORE
than they do.

—ELBERT HUBBARD

THE IMPORTANCE OF COMMITMENT

⊰ ⊱

Most of us look for something that will make a difference in our lives. Many, if not most of us, would like to live lives that make a positive difference in the world in which we live.

Sheila Bethal, a professional business speaker, put it this way:

"We all want to be inspired, motivated and encouraged to do our best."

The secret to this kind of fulfilling life is commitment ... commitment to a mission. If you would like to excel in life, to be the best that you can be (and who wouldn't) then commit yourself to the task of developing your skills, talents and abilities to their fullest...

... then put them to work,

... not only in the development of a great career, but also in the many tasks necessary to make your community the best it can be, reaching out to the poor,

... the uneducated

... the sick and

... infirm

uplifting yourself as you lift them from their desperate circumstances.

The key to excellent
PERFORMANCE
is this:
MOBILIZE
your intellect
AND SKILLS....
then demand
THE BEST
from them.

— W.A.

DEFEATING FEAR

❧ ❧

One of our late, great Presidents stated:

"The only thing we have to fear is fear itself."

Perhaps this great leader understood how dangerous and self-defeating fear can be. Fear is an emotional cancer that eats away at our potential, rendering us incapable of overcoming life's challenges ... robbing us in advance of the successes we so deeply desire!

The first step toward conquering fear is action. When we challenge our fears we defeat them. Ralph Waldo Emerson said, "Do the thing we fear, and the death of fear is certain." Tom Hopkins the great corporate trainer suggests: "Do what you fear most and you control fear."

Dale Carnegie, author of *How to Win Friends and Influence People*, said, "Do the thing that you fear to do and keep on doing it ... that is the quickest and surest way ever yet discovered to conquer fear."

The second most important step in dealing with fear is knowledge. Therefore, commit yourself to the acquisition of knowledge. For you know it will dispel the fears that would overcome you. Earl Nightingale said, "Whenever we are afraid it is because we don't know enough." Ignorance begets fear. Education and knowledge defeat fear and give birth to courage and confidence ... the courage and confidence one needs to accept the challenges that are a part of everyday life.

Quitters
NEVER WIN
and winners
NEVER QUIT.

— Unknown

OVERCOMING THE IMPOSSIBLE

❧ ❧

There was a man in the history of our country who was labeled the greatest agricultural scientist this country has ever produced. He is credited with single-handedly transforming the pattern of agriculture throughout the south. Talk about meeting challenges or overcoming obstacles, this man started out as a slave!! At 13 years of age he became a free man, with no education, but a burning desire to learn ...
... and learn, he did!!

This man was none other than George Washington Carver. It is said that in spite of the humiliations of unspeakable discrimination, he continued to work tirelessly toward the attainment of his goals. It is obvious that goals were vital to his achievement.

He was ultimately invited to testify before the United States Congress. He made one statement that should be important to all of us:
"Life requires thorough preparation. We must rid ourselves of the idea that there is a short cut to achievement ..."

Perhaps the lesson to be learned here is that impossible obstacles can be overcome if we have both the goals and the desire.

Don't complain about what you do not have. Take the abilities you do have and put them to work to acquire what you want in life.

If you don't
have a
DESTINATION,
you will never
GET THERE.

—Harvey Mackay

THE MASTER SKILL

❧ ❧

There is a book written by Tom Hopkins entitled *How to Master the Art of Selling* in which he titles one chapter "The Most Necessary Skill Of All."

When one thinks of success one immediately reflects on the many qualities necessary to create a successful person. Some of those qualities might be courage, persistence, dedication, commitment. I am sure you can think of more. However, this excellent volume refers to one simple step as the most necessary skill of all to achieve success.

What is the most necessary skill of all? Goals and goal setting. Dennis Kimbro in his outstanding volume refers to goal setting as "THE MASTER SKILL." His observation is:

> "It is a quality without which no man can attain riches or outstanding success. The man or woman on the move is the person who is intensely goal oriented."

It has always surprised me that as I worked my way through high school, college and graduate school that there was never a course titled "Blueprint For Life." There was never a wise professor amongst the many at whose feet I sat who talked about the importance of goals.

For that reason, I find it necessary to repeat time and again the importance of creating goals, writing them down, vividly picturing them in one's mind and bending every talent and effort in the direction of achieving those goals. If you want to find great satisfaction in life set goals, and achieve them. For it is the achievement of goals that creates life's greatest satisfaction.

Whatever is at
THE CENTER
of our life will be
THE SOURCE
of our security,
GUIDANCE,
wisdom, and power.

—STEPHEN COVEY

THE POWER OF FAITH

◀ ▶

Do you have any idea of how important it is for you to believe in yourself and your ability. If you believe in your own effectiveness ...

If you believe you can do any task ...
this very faith will empower you to greater achievement.

Belief in your ability to succeed enhances dramatically your actual success.

All real motivation starts from within. If you have faith in yourself – in your talents, your skill, your abilities – this will be the source of your strongest motivation to succeed.

Take an inventory of what you have in terms of education, experience, knowledge and skill. These are the resources available to you to achieve whatever success you are looking for.

Then take these resources and allocate them to every task, every opportunity or every challenge that comes your way. As you apply these resources to each of your goals you will also be developing a perceived probability of success. As each goal is accomplished there will develop a feeling of confidence and a sense of achievement that will empower you to your next level of success.

Seek first to
UNDERSTAND,
then to be understood.
THIS PRINCIPLE
is the key to
EFFECTIVE
interpersonal
COMMUNICATION.

—STEPHEN COVEY

MEASURING PERFORMANCE

❧ ❧

Do you think that golf or bowling would be as much fun if we didn't keep score? I can't imagine two basketball or baseball teams competing against each other without keeping score. This idea highlights the importance of MEASURING PERFORMANCE.

One of my favorite phrases as a management executive is
"What gets measured gets done."

This concept is important for each of us in order to determine the progress that we are making in our lives, particularly in our careers. Since constant growth is so important, measuring our success or our growth is extremely important.

Check your goals at the end of each day ...
Check the tasks you had hoped to perform on that given day ...
Compare what you accomplished with what you had set your sights on accomplishing. Constantly measure results against goals. This is what will drive you to greater achievement. Knowing that you may not have achieved everything you wanted in a given day, but that you have in fact accomplished many of your goals, will drive you toward greater achievement the following day. Constantly monitor and measure your progress remembering,
"What gets measured gets done."

The secret to
BECOMING
confident is
PREPARATION.
By practicing we
come to a point of
COMPETENCE.

—W. DAVIS

ACHIEVING EXCELLENCE

❖ ❖

People who are singled out as being the best at what they do are very proud of this designation. Achieving this level of excellence requires some important steps.

First of all, it requires going far beyond the call of duty. Secondly, excellence requires maintaining the highest standards in whatever task we are trying to perform.

The reason we need to focus on excellence is because our opportunities are enhanced in every area of endeavor if we are labeled a person who is committed to being the best.

One of the leading brokers in our country points out:
> "All successful employers are stalking men who will do the unusual, men who think, men who attract attention by performing more than is expected of them."

This the lesson: Every job is a self-portrait of the person who did it.

My advice: Autograph your work with excellence.

Concentration is the
MAGIC KEY
that opens
THE DOOR
to accomplishment.

—W. DAVIS

THE IMPORTANCE OF DECISIVENESS

❧ ❧

Most top executives are very decisive people. When action is demanded they do not allow an important decision to hang in limbo.

In a study that I recently read, three-fourths of executives made decisions with their heads. Some made decisions with their hearts, but the special few VERY SUCCESSFUL executives used both their heads and their hearts.

Decision making is an important key to success.
Here are three steps that will enable you to be an effective decision maker.

First, gather information to learn all available options.
Second, think through all of the options. If I make a decision what will be the result?
Third, to make successful decisions you must avoid decisions based on fear since fear does not bring good results.

Finally, base your decisions on conviction. Believe that your decision will bring positive results. Believe that your decision will fill the specific need intended. Remember, to get the desired results every decision must be made on facts.

Your chances of
SUCCESS IN
any undertaking can
ALWAYS BE
measured by
YOUR BELIEF IN
yourself.

—R. COLLIER

DETERMINATION

❧ ❧

In a world filled with tempting distractions, staying the course you have outlined for yourself is increasingly challenging. This is where

DETERMINATION

becomes a vitally important factor for success.

A characteristic of highly successful people is that nothing can deter them from their chosen path. Their determination never flags! All high achievers work with a relentless determination to reach their goals.

Successful people understand that there will be obstacles, large and small, and there will be difficulties in the path of their success. However, not only are the successful willing to pay the high price of achievement, but they also are so heavily committed to their goals that they will not quit until they are accomplished.

Take this suggestion home with you: "Let nothing deter you from your goals." Expect problems and obstacles as part of the process. As you overcome each obstacle with unflagging determination remember this great thought:
"There is no success without hardship."

Our minds,
OUR THOUGHTS
and our reactions
DETERMINE
our attitude. We can
RESPOND
negatively or
POSITIVELY.

—W.A.

THE POWER OF HAPPINESS

✄ ✄

Did you know that happy people are far more successful that unhappy people? Happy people are also more optimistic, which results, believe it or not, in better health. In addition, happy, optimistic people succeed in business far more than pessimistic people.

The question is, "Can we affect our own happiness?" "Can we make ourselves happier?" Can we develop the "happiness habit?"
The answer to that question is: YES. We do have the power to improve our happiness by the way we act today.

Our actions leave a residue within us, so by acting in the way happy people act it is possible for us to make ourselves into happier people. For example, if you act optimistic you will end up developing that trait. Act happy and you will become happy!

The bottom line is this: One way to become a happy person is to act like one ...
... Remembering that happiness is also a characteristic for success. Cultivate happiness and you will discover that it will produce positive results in your life and your career.

The more you
CAN DREAM,
the more you
CAN DO.

—MICHAEL KORDA

THE IMPORTANCE OF SELF-ESTEEM

⋆ ⋆

An important characteristic not often thought about when talking about success is the critical nature of self-esteem. People who love themselves, who believe in themselves, and who have confidence in themselves are people who have the basic foundation on which to build success.

While it is important for others to have faith in you and believe in your abilities, the first most important step is for you to believe in yourself. Conversely, people who have low self-esteem and do not like themselves will be much more susceptible to psychological disorders and will be much less likely to succeed in whatever they try to do.

This is the lesson: Develop a positive outlook based on your own genuine achievement of goals. Look in the mirror every morning and say "I like myself. I believe in myself! I am fun to be with. I have good ideas." Out of this approach will grow the self-esteem necessary to empower you to the level of achievement you desire.

Cherish
YOUR VISIONS
and your
DREAMS,
as they are the
BLUEPRINTS
of your ultimate
ACHIEVEMENTS.

—Napoleon Hill

MORE ON LEARNING

❧ ❧

With all of the persuasiveness at my command let me point out to each of you the importance of learning. As each new day dawns in your life, it needs to be viewed as another day of opportunity to learn.

While most of us have a variety of methods that we use to learn new things on a regular basis, let me give you a suggestion made by Dr. James Lundy who wrote the book titled LEAD, FOLLOW, OR GET OUT OF THE WAY. In it he gives this title to one chapter:

FOUR POWERFUL WORDS

What do you think those four powerful words are? He referred to them as the finest training program in the world per word. The four most powerful words that he is talking about are:

"ASK QUESTIONS AND LISTEN."

In business or in private life the most powerful guideline on how to inspire ...

... how to learn and

...how to guide

almost certainly has to be:

"ASK QUESTIONS AND LISTEN."

Service is the
ESSENCE
of greatness.
ALL GREAT
men and women
BECAME GREAT
because they gave
SOME SPECIAL
service to others.

—W. DAVIS

THE NECESSITY OF RISKS

❧ ❧

Ordinary life is fraught with a wide variety of risks. For example, every farmer must believe when he is planting seeds during the planting season that the proper weather will ensue so that he will have a crop to reap at the end of the growing season. Every friendship requires a belief in a mutual commitment between friends. Every business arrangement entails the acceptance of statements of faith. I must believe that the person I am buying from will deliver as per his verbal commitment.

These are just a few of the risks that one takes in a normal day. More importantly, however, is the fact that the greater the risk the greater the potential opportunity. The bottom line is everyone needs to have faith,

    ... faith in the fact that if we take a chance on planting that crop

        ... if we invest in that business

           ... if we buy that product

we will get the desired results.

Don't be afraid to take risks. Risks are as much a part of life as opportunities. Every relationship and every business opportunity is fraught with risks. Understanding this will enable us to rise above the potential failures that might occur were we to choose to play it safe and take not chances at all.

Success on any
MAJOR SCALE
requires you to accept
RESPONSIBILITY ....
the one quality that all
SUCCESSFUL
people have ....
IS THE ABILITY
to take on
RESPONSIBILITY.

—MICHAEL KORDA

INVESTING YOUR WEALTH

❧ ❧

What does your real wealth consist of? Most people in answer to that question would immediately begin to tabulate their possessions:

> house, car, property, savings and so forth.

However, your real wealth consists of the intellect, abilities and talents with which you were blessed at birth. These are your possessions that no one can take from you. In addition, these possessions are the source of all of your wealth. They need to be invested wisely in whatever career is the one of your choice.

While every person is blessed with varying degrees of intellectual and physical capacity, these gifts if invested wisely and energetically in careers and opportunities of your choice will deliver outstanding results.

Conversely, when these natural abilities and talents are not invested and are left unused, they will disappear.

Enormously successful people are those who recognize where their wealth lies and they develop and invest it wisely. As these gifts are developed they enable the successful to cope with every problem ... overcome every obstacle ... meet every challenge that are a part of every person's life. This then is the secret to personal success:

> "To be what we are, and to become what we are capable of becoming, is the only end of life."

The ability
TO ACCEPT
responsibility is
THE MEASURE
of the man.

—R. Smith

LIMITLESS ACHIEVEMENT

❧ ❧

There is absolutely no limit to what you can achieve. The reason people do not achieve the simplest of goals is, first of all, they do not set their goals and, second of all, they do not really believe in their own hearts that their goals are achievable. As a result, their lives are one failure on top of the other until they reach the point of desperation and hopelessness. It is this kind of thinking that makes up the atmosphere and the environment of the depressed ghetto areas in our major cities.

People there limit themselves with their beliefs, do not make a commitment to rise above the level of their terrible existence, and do not mobilize the gifts that they have, focusing them on achieving their cherished dreams.

The challenge is clear. First of all, take your natural gifts and develop them to the highest possible degree. You do this through study, effort and practice. Second, apply all that you have learned, all the talents that you have developed to every challenge that comes your way. Third, prepare your list of goals making them very high goals, very challenging goals. Then put all of your mobilized gifts together, applying them to the goals that will raise your life to its highest possible level of achievement.

Don't fall into the trap of assuming that you're AUTOMATICALLY "entitled" to pay INCREASES, promotions, even your job .... Even if you PERFORM WELL. The best thing you can do is constantly upgrade your skills ....

—PRICE PRITCHETT

THE MEANING OF PERSISTENCE

❧ ❧

James J. Corbett, the great heavyweight champion who finally defeated the legendary John L. Sullivan in the ring, made a statement I like:

> "You become a champion by fighting one more round. When things are tough, you fight one more round."

We have talked about persistence previously, what is important is to understand that without persistence most projects would end of in failure. It appears that Jim Corbett understood this.

Persistence carries with it enormous power. Society believes in people with unlimited persistence because it knows the person with persistence will never stop short of his objective. Dennis Kimbro says:

> "Nothing will take the place of persistence. A person who refuses to quit and keeps going in the face of insuperable obstacles is the person who will succeed on every level."

Persistence is the key to success. It is a never-quit attitude. It is endurance. It is perseverance. It is determination all wrapped up into one dynamic force. Persistence will empower you to overcome every obstacle in your search for success and meaning in your life.

Knowledge
IS POWER!

— PRESIDENT GEORGE W. BUSH

ON BEING DIFFERENT

❧ ❧

Those who set themselves apart from the crowd usually become leaders. They become the pace setters ... the people who everyone wishes to emulate.

Differentiation, of course, is an extremely important concept in business. However, it is no less important a concept in individual life. Those who differentiate themselves from the crowd tend to accomplish more, reach their goals, and influence their world in a positive way. The following steps will help you set yourself apart from the crowd:

Always deliver more than you promise!

Always go the extra mile!

Always demand the best from yourself!

Since most seem to do only what is necessary to get by, those who stand out, who are different, are those who do that something extra making them more valuable both to their society and to the business in which they work.

Finally, if you want to set yourself apart mobilize all of your abilities and bring them to focus on every opportunity,

... every challenge

... every obstacle.

Those who are different in this way are the ones who succeed. They are the ones who will achieve their most important goals.

I believe that
EVERY RIGHT
implies a
RESPONSIBILITY;
every opportunity,
AN OBLIGATION;
every possession,
A DUTY.

—JOHN D. ROCKEFELLER

WHAT DO YOU VALUE?

❈ ❧

While reading Sheila Bethel's book titled *MAKING A DIF-FERENCE*, I read a statement that hit me right between the eyes. The statement was: "We are what we value!"

What powerful questions this statement raises. For example,
WHAT DO YOU VALUE?
Do you value commitment ...
    ... achievement,
        ... integrity,
            ... productivity?

If you are like most people you want to find fulfillment in your work. Most people want to be inspired and feel a part of something that matters. If you want to make your life more meaningful what you value will make a vital difference in your life.

My suggestion is:
    "These are the characteristics that we need to value, namely, achievement, commitment to excellence,
    ...honesty,
        ... hard work,
            ... a caring attitude toward all fellow workers and fellow human beings ...
... Remembering at all times that <u>we are what we value</u> ... and what we value will make the difference between an empty life and one filled with satisfaction and achievement.

Every single employee SHOULD ASSUME personal RESPONSIBILITY for upgrading his or her job performance. Your PRODUCTIVITY, response time, quality, cost control, and customer service should all show steady gains. And your skills should be in a state of constant renewal.

— PRICE PRITCHETT

THE IMPORTANCE OF QUESTIONS

⊰ ⊱

One of America's most famous physicists tells this story of his childhood. When he came home from school, his mother would ask him, "Did you ask any good questions today?" He attributed a great deal of his success to his ability to ask good questions.

Perhaps this is in keeping with the proverb that goes, "If you know all the answers, you haven't asked all the questions."

One of the less frequently used secrets to success is taking the time to conceive and formulate important and meaningful questions ... questions that will open the doors to more specific knowledge required to develop greater achievement.

The lesson here is very important: develop the ability to ask questions and then listen carefully to the answers. Since learning involves the answering of all sorts of important questions your ability to ask the right questions will be vital to your success.

Developing your personal ability to ask meaningful questions will move you in the direction of acquiring greater and greater knowledge, which in turn will translate into superior success and achievement.

Failure teaches you
NOT TO FEAR
failure, because if you
CAN SURVIVE
it to fight again, you
HAVEN'T FAILED.
You have heightened
your appreciation
OF SUCCESS.

—HARVEY MACKAY

LIVING THE MOMENT AT HAND

❧ ❧

Many years ago the late, great Nat King Cole recorded a beautiful song titled "For All We Know We May Never Meet Again." More recently another great performer, Whitney Houston, recorded a song titled "One Moment In Time."

Somewhat by accident I heard these two songs on the same day while traveling through the south and it reminded me of the fact that we as individuals tend to look back (sometimes with regret) and look forward to some future event failing many times to give the proper attention to the moment at hand.

Someone once said, "Dreaming of a false past keeps an enormous number of people from moving effectively in the present."

The great corporate sales trainer, Tom Hopkins, stresses the importance of "living the moment at hand." What he is referring to is taking full advantage of what is happening TODAY.

Apply your wisdom, talents and skills to the challenges of the moment. Ask yourself "What needs to be done today?" Yesterday has passed! You can't change it! Tomorrow may never happen.

Those who want success, and who achieve great success are those who live the fullest in the moment at hand. They are the ones who do not worry about the past or the future but confront each opportunity and challenge as it comes.

Few of us lead
UNBLEMISHED
personal or professional
lives. It's the
ABILITY TO
overcome our faults,
RATHER THAN
never to
EXPERIENCE
them, that counts.

—HARVEY MACKAY

RESPONSIBILITY

⋊ ⋉

I recently received a call from a young man who is in the securities business. He has heard this program frequently and he called me to share with me an important thought.

He said he had been thinking about what sets apart the leader,
     ... the president of the company,
         ... the entrepreneur,
            ... the CEO from the ordinary workman
or more accurately from the individual who merely wants a job and a salary. After giving it much thought he said that it occurred to him there is one word separating the two and his feeling was that one word is RESPONSIBILITY.

He is absolutely correct.
If you are looking for success,
     ... for leadership,
         ... for fulfillment
if you are looking for a position that makes you feel what you do matters, then you must have the willingness to accept responsibility.

Michael Corda said, "Success on any major scale requires you to accept responsibility ... In the final analysis, the one quality that all successful people have ... is the ability to take on responsibility."

Do the
COMMON
thing
UNCOMMONLY
well.

— PAUL OREFFICE

ACCOUNTABILITY

❧ ❧

Many years ago Life Magazine ran an editorial title "Let George Do It." In it the observation was made that too many people in our country wanted to avoid accountability letting someone else do the job that they themselves should have done. It was viewed as a major developing problem.

Have you ever noticed how many people do not want to accept accountability for their actions? Many today want to blame all sorts of extenuating circumstances whether they be environmental or hereditary for their predicament or their nefarious actions.

The question of accountability is a very serious one. People who are searching for success will always assume accountability for what they do. A key characteristic of successful people is that they consider themselves 100 percent accountable for their actions. Very successful people do not make excuses for their mistakes.

The bottom line is this: You are accountable for your deeds. Don't pass the buck, blaming circumstances or environment for your predicament. Assume full accountability for your actions. For this is the attitude that will mark you for superior success and achievement. People who accept accountability are the leaders in business and politics, applying their talents to meeting the demanding challenges of life.

Being
MISERABLE
is a habit;
BEING HAPPY
is a habit; and the
CHOICE
is yours.

—TOM HOPKINS

KNOWLEDGE AND CHANGE

❧ ❧

While great knowledge will not guarantee success, it is nevertheless true that the more you know the more effective you will be in your chosen career. Perhaps this is why one of the major characteristics of extremely high achievers is their commitment to learning!

Remember the old proverb that goes: "You can't teach an old dog new tricks." Not only is this ancient saying incorrect, but I can just imagine how many people placed limits on their careers as the years went by, because they were convinced they could not learn something new.

Learning and study, which is the primary source of knowledge, is the most effective means for dealing with our dynamically changing environment.

"Progress is impossible without change," said George Bernard Shaw, "... and those who cannot change their minds cannot change anything."

Success cannot be achieved without the willingness to change ... and knowledge acquired through learning opens the mind to the changing opportunities and new horizons constantly coming our way.
Make this promise to yourself:

"I will commit myself to daily learning and study. For I realize this is what prepares me for a changing environment and equips me for superior achievement and success."

But it isn't
FAILURE THAT
hurts us most –
FEAR OF FAILURE
does the greatest
DAMAGE.

—Tom Hopkins

WHAT DO YOU HONOR

❖ ❖

Plato once said that "a society cultivates whatever is honored there." Wouldn't it be interesting to examine our lives on the basis of what we honor?

Successful life will depend to a great degree on what we honor. The question that we need to ask ourselves is, "What do WE honor?" What do YOU honor? Do you honor commitment? Honesty? Learning? Study? Hard work?

In his book on leadership, Max DePree says, "Let us make no mistake about what we honor." He was referring to the culture that develops within a company. He went on to say that "a company's values are it's lifeblood."

If it is true that a company consists primarily of people, then the values honored by the company you work for become the values that you honor as an individual.

If we are looking to make our lives productive, we need to honor the right things ... such as honesty, commitment, learning.

We need to educate ourselves. The word "educate" comes from two Latin words, namely, "to lead out, or to draw out." We need to draw out of ourselves through education, the personal qualities that will empower us toward a successful and honorable life.

You are who
YOU THINK
you are, so begin
THINKING THAT
you are who you
WANT TO BE.

—TOM HOPKINS

MORE ON DETERMINATION

❧ ❧

Do you realize how important determination is? Every successful person has had to fight through numerous failures to achieve that success! Most people simply quit ... often just before crossing the final line.

When writing about a commander in the Spanish Civil War, Ernest Hemingway said that he "never knew when everything was lost and if it was, he would fight out of it."

This is the kind of attitude that is characteristic of successful people. They always hang in there. They never give up no matter how bleak the outlook!! They always fight on !!

It is precisely this never-give-up attitude that gives

> Courage ...
>> Strength ...
>>> Vitality and
>>>> Power ...

Power to overcome every failure or barrier that stands between you and your fondest ambitions.

Each of us would do well to cherish and remember this observation by Napoleon Hill, author of *Think and Grow Rich.* who said,

"Effort only fully releases its rewards after a person refuses to quit."

No one can
TEACH YOU
that which
THEY HAVE
not done.

—Tom Hopkins

DEALING WITH ADVERSITY

❧ ❧

One of the unique characteristics of highly successful people is that they believe everything happens for a reason and a purpose, including adversity. They look for the positive results that can come from adversity. They have the ability to focus on what is possible in a highly negative situation. They believe that every adversity contains the seeds of a benefit.

All people who produce outstanding results think precisely this way. Napoleon Hill taught that there is the seed of an equal or greater benefit in every adversity.

How you deal with adversity will determine the degree of your success. It takes great discipline to be able to learn new possibilities from the negatives and failures that are a part of life.

One wise man said, "You CAN drown out the discouraging silent voices that speak in your mind – those voices that hold you back and stifle your creativity and momentum."

Believe that anything is possible. Believe that you can cope with any adversity ...
For belief in limits creates limited people.

Tony Robbins sums it up: "If you have a strong belief in possibility, it is likely you'll achieve it."

Effective change is not
SOMETHING
you do to people.
IT'S SOMETHING
you do with them.

—KEN BLANCHARD

THE TRUTH ABOUT ACCOUNTABILITY

❧ ❧

Have you ever noticed how the powers that be (whether city, state or federal) and the press continually make excuses for every conceivable evil deed! Our society seems to be distorting our laws to favor the criminal and deprive the victim!! For example:

Angry mobs destroy a city! Excuse: They were disadvantaged.

Two children murder their parents! Excuse: They were abused.

A thief is caught burglarizing a supermarket! Excuse: He was poor all his life.

Interestingly, most wealthy, successful people started out as very poor people.

I am here to tell you that success has never been built on a foundation of excuses. We are ACCOUNTABLE for our actions. If you have been a failure in your career,

if you can't get along with people,

if you think you never get a break,

don't make excuses, rather look in the mirror and say to yourself

"I am accountable ...

... My success is my responsibility ...

It is a responsibility I cannot delegate to someone else."

Don't make excuses for your failure. Learn from that failure. Take your talents whatever they may be and put them to work to acquire the success which is your heart's desire. Support your talents with hard work and commitment, always reminding yourself that you are accountable for your failures ... as well as your successes.

While you wait for a
FAVORABLE
opportunity, push
YOURSELF HARD
to increase your
KNOWLEDGE.

—Tom Hopkins

WHAT SUCCESSFUL PEOPLE SEE

❧ ❧

When we talk about vision we are using a word that has two very different meanings. The first meaning of vision is "eyesight." With eyesight you are able to see a beautiful sunset, a beautiful woman, a beautiful flower. The other definition of vision is "insight or perception."

This is what is meant by the ancient Biblical maxim: "Where there is no vision, the people perish." Where there is no perception, no insight, no understanding the people perish. Where there is no perception, insight, understanding, there is no success!

When one observes successful people one discovers that they have a vision that is unique. Successful people do not see failure. On the other hand, they focus with intense concentration on results. If they do not succeed in accomplishing a certain goal, they do not see it as a failure, but see it rather as a learning experience or a stepping-stone to a new level of accomplishment. Superior achievers never see failure. They see opportunities ... learning experiences.

In a world where we are taught to fear failure, those who lead, those who succeed, who achieve greatness are those who do not fear failure. They understand Harvey MacKay's observation: "Tolerate failure ... It is the price of success." The vision of successful people is that they see results, challenges, and achievements.

The simple believeth
EVERY WORD;
but the
PRUDENT MAN
looketh well to
HIS GOING.

—THE BIBLE

FOCUS – KEY TO SUCCESS

❧ ❧

Dr. David Banner, a professor of leadership at the University of the Pacific in Stockton, California, made this interesting observation about people who achieve great success. He pointed out that there is one trait common to all such people, namely, their unique ability to stay focused on their major goal.

For extremely successful people this focus covers three areas. The first area is their thoughts. Remembering the axiom "you become what you think," your thoughts are an extremely important part of your personal effectiveness. Whatever you think about expands in your mind. Your dominant thoughts, when focused, project a clear picture of your purpose ... your goal!

The second area where this focus comes into play is with your intellect ... your brainpower ... your mind. Applying the computer-like power of your mind to whatever problem or challenge that presents itself, will inevitably enable you to deal successfully as each of these opportunities present themselves.

The third area where this focus comes into play is with your physical strength and energy. Great success will require each of us to focus the enormous power of our strength and energy to meet our desired goals.

The difference between successful and unsuccessful people can often be seen in the successful persons ability to feed his mind on positive rather than negative goals.

A daily threat to or positive mindset is the negativism that is such a part of today's world. To deal with this and to avoid a life of fear, scarcity and despair, Dr. Banner suggests we focus our minds on those positive goals and purposes that will elevate us to our greatest achievement!

With all
THY GETTING,
get understanding.

—Forbes Magazine

THE SUCCESS RECIPE

❧ ❧

One of the great success stories of all time is that of the late Dave Thomas, founder of Wendy's. He learned very early about the negative side of life. He never knew his birth parents and his adoptive mother died when he was only five years old. As a very young child, he moved frequently from state to state as his adoptive father sought work.

"It wasn't easy," said Dave. "No roots; no sense of belonging. With all that moving I didn't get a chance to know kids. I guess that's why work became my constant companion."

At age 12 he got a job delivering groceries. Fired from that job he landed another at a drugstore and was fired again when the boss found out that he wasn't 16.

When he was 15 his family moved to Fort Wayne, Indiana, where be became a busboy in a local restaurant. When his family moved again, Dave decided to stay in Fort Wayne. He took a room at the YMCA and dropped out of school after the tenth grade. Working late at the restaurant, he was simply to tired too study.

Dave met Colonel Harland Sanders several years later when his boss bought a franchise from the Kentucky Colonel. His boss offered him a deal. Take over the management of four struggling Kentucky Fried Chicken stores, turn them around and pay off the $200,000 in debt. The reward: 45% ownership. He promoted the stores tirelessly! By 1968 he had turned them around and sold them back to Kentucky Fried Chicken for $1.5 million.

Today, Dave's chain of Wendy's has grown from a single operation to 3,800 restaurants worldwide. Now this is the clincher! What was Dave's recipe for success? Answer: "Hard work, honesty and total commitment." Dave's observation: "Like Napoleon Hill said, you can have anything you want if you set your goals high enough."

Before you can
ATTAIN SUCCESS,
the effort
YOU'RE MAKING
to get it has to be
WORTHY OF
what you want.

—TOM HOPKINS

THE POWER OF BELIEFS

❧ ❧

Have you ever thought of what drives you to do the things that you do? Have you ever said to yourself, "What made me do that?" or "Why did I say that?" Perhaps you are wondering about the answer to these questions?

Well, here is the answer: It is your beliefs that move you in one direction or another, that drive you to challenge and accomplish great goals. It is your beliefs that empower you!

One of the great football coaches of all time put it more accurately. His name is Don Shula. He said, "Your beliefs are what make things happen. Beliefs come true. Inadequate beliefs are set-ups for inadequate performance." The bottom line is your beliefs are the most important aspect of your intellectual process.

For example, if you firmly believe you can overcome what appears to be an impossible obstacle, you probably can. If you believe that you can successfully perform your duties in a given job, you probably will. If you believe in your ability to succeed in almost anything that you attempt, you no doubt will succeed.

So, then, carefully examine what you believe about life, about career, about yourself! For your beliefs will empower you to accomplish your goals. Behind all your accomplishments are the power of your beliefs.

Therefore, be very careful what you believe. For not only are your beliefs at the heart of your being, but they are also the core of your value system that will drive you in the direction of success or failure.

You will never
FLY WITH
the eagles if you
SPEND ALL
your time
ASSOCIATING
with the turkeys.

—W.A.

YOU ARE SOMEBODY

❧ ❧

Recently a young employee of mine knocked on my office door. I looked up from my desk and said, "Who is it?" He replied, "It's only me. I'm nobody." I reacted immediately and perhaps somewhat angrily saying, "Don't ever say that again. You are somebody very important."

This small anecdote illustrates a common problem, namely, low self-esteem! We must remember that what we mentally project reproduces in kind.

Negative thinking produces debilitating, negative results. Tell yourself you are "nobody" and it will become a self-fulfilling prophecy. Positive thinking, on the other hand, sets in motion positive, creative forces. The result: success flows toward you.

Deep in the heart of every individual is a vast reservoir of untapped power. This largely untapped power exists in the form of talent, intellect and ability ...
   ... and herein lies one's potential to be somebody. Most people tap into only a small part of this power ... in most cases using less than 10 percent of it, thus guaranteeing mediocrity!

Why don't you make a commitment to dig deep into these powerful resources in your own heart! If you do, I will guarantee you a life of success and fulfillment. No, you will not just be anybody, YOU WILL BE SOMEBODY!

If "society" is
RESPONSIBLE
for everything,
then no one is
PERSONALLY
responsible
FOR ANYTHING.

—Newt Gingrich

MORE ON THE EXTRA MILE

❧ ❧

Many an employee has wondered, I am sure, why he did-n't receive a certain promotion ... or that long expected raise. This happens regularly in the workplace. Maybe this has happened to you!

Perhaps you need to be reminded of that important obser-vation made by a very perceptive journalist: "If you don't do any more than you are paid for, you'll never get paid for any more than you do."

This brings up the subject of commitment, or going the extra mile ...

... and this is the point at which you separate the successful from the unsuccessful ...

... the high achievers from the mediocre performers.

Those who receive that promotion or that long expected raise are the ones who GO THE EXTRA MILE.

Dr. Ken Blanchard co-author of *The One Minute Manager,* a book that remained on the New York Times best-seller list for 12 months, puts it very precisely when he says,
"One trait that distinguishes successful people from unsuccessful people is a willingness to go the extra mile – to do what others are not willing to do."
There is no secret to great success! It's very simple! Very uncomplicated!!
In everything you do, GO THE EXTRA MILE!

The pursuit of
HAPPINESS
is not defined by
THE GROUP
you came from but by
THE DREAM
you seek and the
DREAMER
you seek it with.

—NEWT GINGRICH

MENTAL ATROPHY

❧ ❧

Some years ago a friend of mine broke his leg, requiring it to be in a cast for quite some time. When the cast was finally removed, his leg had noticeably shrunk in size. The muscles and the tissue atrophied, the doctor said, because it was totally immobile.
To build the leg back to its former size would require a lengthy period of regular exercise.

It has been my observation that many people reduce their opportunities for success because they experience MEN-TAL ATROPHY. This condition is the direct result of a major lack of intellectual exercise.

These people never read a book ...
    ... refuse to study ...
        ... make no attempt to learn ...
            ... do not even read the daily newspaper!
They seem to refuse to expose their minds to new ideas. More than any other condition, this attitude guarantees failure!

One of the more important keys to success is the willing-ness to learn something new at every opportunity ...
... and to realize that it is in constant learning that success lies. For a mind challenged by studying and learning will always expand to receive it. It is a mind thus challenged that is prepared to meet every opportunity ... overcome every obstacle on the road to success. Perhaps Oliver Wendell Holmes knew something about this when he said, "Man's mind stretched to a new idea never goes back to its original dimensions."

A wise man
WILL HEAR,
and will increase
LEARNING;
and a man of
UNDERSTANDING
shall attain unto
WISE COUNSELS.

—THE BIBLE

LIFE IS NOT A LOTTERY

◆ ◆

A leading politician recently suggested in a speech, widely quoted by the press, that success or failure depends on how you have been treated by "life's lottery." The implication in this statement is that success or failure is a result of luck or chance.

This thought is totally alien to all observable facts!! Success is not a matter of chance.

More often than not it is the result of hard work and total commitment.

Far less than 1 percent of all millionaires had their wealth given to them! A minuscule minority of the millions of people in this country have inherited sufficient wealth to make them millionaires.

If you could talk to David Thomas ... founder of Wendy's, currently with 3,800 locations, Or Ray Kroc ... founder of McDonald's or Sam Walton founder of WalMart, the world's largest retailer ...

You would find them in total agreement on one important point. All of these exceptionally successful people would agree on this important point. Success, more than anything else, is the result of hard work!!

Each of these men started out with little or nothing in terms of wealth. Dave Thomas was an orphan who went on his own at age 16 years, living at the YMCA in Fort Wayne, Indiana. His recipe for success was "hard work, honesty and total commitment." Sam Walton put it this way- "Honesty and hard work."

Burn this fact in your mind. You are not the victim of some fickle fate or random lottery.
What you are ... And what you become will depend on you ... On your willingness to develop your talents and intellect ... On your willingness to apply them to your desired goals.

You will always maximize your personal success,

Whatever your personal definition of that term might be, Through study, hard work and total commitment to your goals.

Like sight,
CREATIVE VISION
and a positive mental
ATTITUDE
are developed skills.
You can
ACQUIRE THEM ...
just like any activity of
THE MIND.

—W. CLEMENT STONE

KEY SOURCES TO PERSONAL POWER

❧ ❧

Have you ever noticed how most successful people exude a certain inexplicable power ...

… When they step up to speak to a group ...

… When they enter a room ...

… When they meet new people?

This personal power didn't just happen! It is the result of several key steps they have taken to enhance their personal power and confidence.

The following are the steps you must take to develop this type of confidence and personal power:

You must become constant learners, absorbing vast amounts of knowledge and information on a wide variety of subjects.

You must work tirelessly at your ability to communicate, constantly enlarging your vocabulary. We communicate with words. Therefore, the understanding and the use of words is the key to effective communication.

You must be incorrigibly enthusiastic. Nothing moves people you are trying to influence more than enthusiasm.

Sam Walton, probably the greatest entrepreneur of the 20th century, could constantly be seen visiting competitor's stores taking notes on a yellow tablet ... always searching for new ideas ... always learning different ways to achieve his goals as America's number one merchant.

If you are looking for success, follow Sam Walton's footsteps, not only in his relentless efforts in accumulating knowledge, but also by emulating his boundless enthusiasm for his work.

LIGHT THE FIRE OF DESIRE

☒ ☒

If you have arrived at this page in reading *Accept the Challenge* you probably have realized that there are three recurring themes in the book that can fuel the deepest desires in your heart ... and please note, every success you achieve begins with a burning desire that cannot be extinguished until that certain success is achieved!

The first theme is learning and knowledge. The accumulation of knowledge both general and specific is an ongoing process. To put it another way, education never stops for the person who seeks outstanding success. For this person, education is a continuing process, a constant ongoing effort, which day-by-day and year-by-year further equips him to achieve his most desired goals.

The second recurring theme is the vital importance of goals without which there will be little or no achievement. Goals enable you to develop a clear understanding of what you wish your destination to be! Carefully crafted goals will give you the direction to achieve that success which is your fondest dream, your deepest desire. They may change somewhat as the years pass, but they will be your mile stones on the road to what you desire as your ultimate achievement in every area of your life.

The third recurring theme is FOCUS. There is a tremendous increase in knowledge acquired through constant learning. This is what better equips one to achieve one's goals. However, it must be totally focused on the goals we want to achieve. Every bit of knowledge, wisdom and skill one accumulates through the continuing learning process must be mobilized and focused on each goal, for these are the stepping stones toward one's ultimate successes. Without focus, the energy of one's accumulated knowledge and skill becomes diffused, losing the concentrated power necessary to drive one towards ultimate achievement.

Finally, at the heart of every great achievement or attainment of a treasured goal is desire. One must have desire! Without desire there is no achievement, no accomplishment of goals. So light the fire of desire and go for your goals! This is the secret! It is where you will find meaningful fulfillment and success.